WHAT PEOPLE ARE SAYING A
AND *ROOMS OF A MOTHER'S HEART...*

Finally! I've been waiting to read this book! I want to learn from a mom who's been there. I want to learn from a mom who's allowed God to re-purpose her pain and grow where she is planted. I want to learn from a mom who will cheer me on with wisdom and grace. Carol McLeod is that mom.

—*Amy Groeschel*
Cofounder, Life.Church
Author; founder, Branch15

Jesus says in John 14:2, "My Father's house has many dwelling places." Carol's key insights and life lessons beautifully unlock the doors into the dwelling places of God's heart—rooms of comfort, assurance, and wisdom for ourselves and our children. Enter into God's shelter and let Carol guide you through "a mother's heart."

—*Kathleen Cooke*
Cofounder, Cooke Media Group and The Influence Lab
Author, *Hope 4 Today*

The principles Carol McLeod shares in this wonderful book offer a soothing balm of insights and guidance for any woman navigating the unique journey of motherhood. Carol's chapter on discipline alone is worth the read. My only regret as I turn the last page is that it wasn't available when I first became a mother. How fortunate for all that it is available now!

—*Cassie Byram*
Founder and CEO, Mamala Media
Creator and producer, Treasure Toons Animation

Motherhood is not for the faint of heart. It's a marathon of laying down your life in favor of your kids, pointing them to the Word of God, and praying for them regularly. In this profound book, Carol offers the wisdom of a mama who continually built her motherhood on the foundation of God's Word. Coming alongside you as a gentle mentor, Carol offers practical suggestions combined with wisdom from the Word of God, to strengthen your soul as a mama. I have watched Carol's life and I can say with certainty that she lives her message! If you want your home filled with joy, this is your book! I highly recommend it!

—*Becky Harling*
Conference speaker; parent coach
Author, *How to Listen So Your Kids Will Talk*

I was told I would never have children. After a chronic battle with endometriosis, medical treatments, and much prayer, God blessed me with the miracle of a daughter and a son. How I wish I had Carol McLeod's book *Rooms of a Mother's Heart* earlier in my life. Her words are rich because they come from a life dedicated to God and the miracle of motherhood. She is the confidante you call on a teary day, the mentor you glean from in an unfamiliar season, and the friend with whom you share your joys and sorrows. This must-have guide is truly a gift, wherever you are in your journey as a mother.

—*Angela Donadio*
Bible teacher; author
Host, *Make Life Matter* podcast

Goodness! Carol's words are absolutely captivating! Her words are going to bring encouragement to mothers everywhere! Carol McLeod is no stranger to the *stretch* we often experience as mamas—whether it's found in our bodies, our hearts, or both. Because of an array of personal experiences, along with Spirit-led insight, *Rooms of a Mother's Heart* is a deep well of timeless wisdom. If you're looking for an honest voice with a side of faith-filled encouragement, Carol is your gal and this is your book.

—*Jenn Jewel*
Pastor's wife
Host, *The Messy Table* podcast

What a lovely, lovely book! *Rooms of a Mother's Heart* is an inspired song of praise for the too-often maligned role of motherhood. I wish I had had it at hand some 25 years ago when, as a confirmed career gal, I was surprised by God's call to adopt a baby girl from China. The day my husband and I brought our daughter home is the day God blessed me with the greatest gift of my life. I take away this thought from Carol's book and treasure it in my heart: "I learned that rocking my baby to sleep was more satisfying than rocking the world with my achievements."

—*Ann Tatlock*
Novelist; editor; children's book author

There is no higher calling than motherhood—and no greater joy—but sometimes that joy arrives with fatigue, worry, and feelings of insecurity because we don't know what to do. In the Bible, God sets the standard for older women to mentor the younger women. Moms, my dear friend, Carol McLeod, will be that voice of wisdom for you. In the pages of *Rooms of a Mother's Heart*, you'll discover the mother God meant you to be, sage advice from a loving mom who's been there and done that, laughter, lists, and much more. You won't learn to become a perfect mom, but you'll leave the pages equipped to be the loving and godly mom you want to be. I highly recommend this book!

—*Michelle Cox*
Bestselling author, *Just 18 Summers*
When God Calls the Heart series

Carol McLeod's unsmotherable optimism, insightful practicality, and infinite spiritual wisdom are just what every mother needs when she feels inadequate, insecure, and discouraged. With utter vulnerability, this book exposes the fears moms try to keep tucked inside their souls. Do you *ever* feel as if you're a good enough mother to the child or children God privileged you to raise? If you are a mom who feels like a failure, find encouragement and comfort in *Rooms of a Mother's Heart*! If you and a couple of friends want to better understand how to become the mom God had in mind when He created your children, read this book together. If you're part of a moms' group, enhance each other's growth and discover your deeper mom potential by discussing *Rooms of a Mother's Heart* in weekly sessions based on each chapter. If you identify as a mom, no matter how you learn from it, this book will lift your spirit and help you celebrate motherhood on a whole new level.

—*Anita Agers-Brooks*
Trauma expert; certified communications specialist
Award-winning author

Drawing upon Scripture, experiential wisdom, and so much more, Carol reminds us, "It is in dying to self that we become significant in the kingdom of our Creator and it is in serving others that we achieve true greatness." Carol gently and directly reminds us that motherhood "is the highest calling a woman embraces." As a mommy of three and grandmommy of three, I've had no greater joy than being a mommy. I wish I had *Rooms of a Mother's Heart* when my children were little. I'm grateful to have it now, to share with it my grandchildren's mommies.

—*Suzanne Kuhn*
Founder and CEO, Brookstone Creative Group

Ever wander into the empty bedroom of your son or daughter for no other reason than to think of them? In this book, thoughts of your children and how to shape their lives are in every room of your home. As I walked with Carol through the rooms of my heart, I wanted to bring other mothers with me. Housemothers, foster and adoptive moms, and even grandmothers raising their grandchildren need the encouragement in these pages! Carol takes us on a tour of your heart's rooms with the most uplifting words. Every woman wearing *mom shoes* will be reminded and assured that she has been handpicked by God to do the extraordinary work of motherhood.

—*Jean Caceres-Gonzalez*
Founder, His House Children's Home, Miami, FL

As an empty-nester, looking back on motherhood can be a mixed bag of emotions, yet I still consider it my highest calling in life. Oh, how I wish this book had been on my bookshelf 26 years ago when I was blessed with my firstborn! Carol shares from her heart with such beautiful honesty that you will be spurred on to see motherhood through a different lens—one of joy and nurture rather than just duty and discipline. No matter what season or *room* of motherhood you are in, this book will be a delight to read!

—*Carrie Kittinger*
Ministry leader; speaker

In this refreshing book, Carol takes us on a journey through *Rooms of a Mother's Heart*. Each room is filled with real life moments, foundational principles, layered with Scriptures, and overflowing with hope for each changing season. Carol writes in such a way that she captures the heart and joys of motherhood while enlarging the vision and sober call of raising the next generation. Her love for God's Word is so evident! She intertwines it in such a powerful way with godly principles, leaving you as the reader with hope and encouragement for each new season. Her transparency and authenticity cause a mother to feel hopeful as she walks through the challenges of motherhood, knowing she is not alone and God will help her. No matter what season of motherhood you are presently in, your heart will be stirred and encouraged with healing hope and a fresh vision to be the godly mother God has called you to be!

—*Diane Zarlengo*
Director of women's ministry
Church prayer coordinator; senior pastor's wife

In exquisite fashion, Carol McLeod combines her three life passions—her deep love of Jesus, her high calling to motherhood, and her exceptional ability to communicate with the written word—to create a life-changing masterpiece to be read by *every* mom! Carol takes her readers on a most beautiful journey through *Rooms of a Mother's Heart*, with priceless nuggets for all moms— from the hopeful and expectant stage of becoming a mom, all the way through to the empty nest stage—and every stage in the middle. Carol opens her heart wide as she shares very personally from the depth of her rich and real-life experiences and from her profound, God-given wisdom. A few promises for the readership of Carol's dream of a book are: (1) you will be stretched and moved to tears of joy again and again as Carol brilliantly weaves in messages of grace, hope, and joy to what otherwise could be seasons of frustration, struggle, and mundane; (2) you will hear from the heart and from the voice of a momma who took her motherhood calling for what it is—of dire importance; (3) you will be introduced to absolutely delightful ideas and tactics for which most moms have not been exposed; and (4) you will immediately want *every mom* in your circle to read Carol's heart through *Rooms of a Mother's Heart* and hear and learn from her gentle, most insightful and learned ways and words. *Rooms of a Mother's Heart* is sure to become a timeless classic to be read by every mother, mother-to-be, and grandmother. Carol McLeod has done it again! Extraordinary!

—*Kim Pickard Dudley*
Founder and principal, The Kim Pickard Dudley Group

Carol is my long-time friend and mentor of all things godly, kind, and wise. Her greatest impact in my life came from observing her as she mothered her children with grace and compassion. The words she has written are the life that she has lived. Biblical truth paired with personal vignettes make *Rooms of a Mother's Heart* meaningful and applicable in your journey as a mother and a Christ-follower. Glimpses of Carol's life will inspire you to be intentional in your role as mother, honing it as a craft. You will see the absolute privilege of this call, the real joy that is available in laying down your life for another, and the remarkable journey of becoming who God designed you to be. As you read *Rooms of a Mother's Heart*, you will learn how to mother with the heart of the Father.

—*Dawn Frink*
Teacher; mentor

What a *joy* it is to call Carol McLeod my dear friend. For forty years, I have watched Carol pour Jesus into each of her five children. Homeschooling, Bible studies, singing, taking the boys to basketball practice, or sitting on the front row at the local children's theater watching her girls sing and dance; every single thing that mattered to Carol's children mattered to Carol. She never missed a moment and she was and continues to be their biggest cheerleader. I remember how Carol cried when she saw a picture of our beautiful baby girl. Carol had prayed me through some difficult days of waiting for *the call* that would let us know we could fly to Guatemala to pick up our five-month-old daughter. Carol told me years ago, "Motherhood is a mission and there is no greater or more fulfilling calling." No truer words have ever been spoken.

—*Lynn Field*
Spring Hill, TN

Carol has been a friend since college. Take a seat on the *front porch* as you read *Rooms of a Mother's Heart* for personal, impacting discovery. Carol's pursuit of God transcends modern philosophy for mothers planting into their children's lives while her captivating storytelling incorporates the poignant application of God's sovereign plan for fruit that will remain.

—*Kit Marshall*
Mayor, Aledo, TX
Emergency management officer

This book should be on every mother's desk! It is very encouraging and at the same time easy to read. Contained in these pages are both help and hope! *Rooms of a Mother's Heart* is at once thought provoking, yet practical. Carol shares her walk with God and the joy of discipling the five blessings that God gave to her. You will be blessed as you read this book and as you continue on your walk of motherhood.

—*Lynn Custer*
Mentor to homeschooling moms over 25 years

Rooms of a Mother's Heart is pure gold. It depicts facets of motherhood I've felt but never heard explained with such clarity. It spoke right to my tired but full momma heart. Carol's wisdom cast comfort into my sticky and beautiful life with toddlers, but also directed such insight to the future. This book transformed my perspective of my role as a mom and impacted how I want to raise our kids.

—*Sierra Forrest*
Founder, Practical Jesus, Inc.

Rooms of a Mother's Heart by Carol McLeod is a book that is desperately needed in today's culture. Her voice is an answered prayer to mothers who are praying for wisdom and discernment in raising their children to be warriors of this generation. Carol has so much insight and experience with both sons and daughters, through all of the seasons of parenting, from the sleepless nights of caring for a newborn to the sleepless nights of coaching a teenager and on to the sweet spots of being a Marmee. Carol has been a dear friend, sister, and mentor to me for over a decade. Reading this book is like sitting across from a dear friend, over a cup of coffee, and gleaning wisdom from someone who has parented five children for the span of 40 years. If you are looking for a book to carry you through the seasons of mothering, this is it!

—*Monica Orzechowski*
Production director, Life Church Buffalo

Carol's books have been a source of joy and inspiration as I've walked through my own journey of motherhood. In Rooms of a Mother's Heart, she throws the curtains wide open to reveal the full view of raising children as God intended. With that, I feel joyful anticipation for what's next as I aim to raise a man close to God's heart.

—*Johanna Stamps*
Author; life coach

As a new mom, this book is exactly what I needed! Carol's decades of wisdom poured out in these pages brought an ease to my soul and encouraged me in my new role as a mother. Her writing is full of biblical truth applied in practical ways. I love the way Carol continually points to Jesus and refocuses the reader's heart on Christ as the center of the home. This will be a book I refer to repeatedly for wisdom and hope in the midst of motherhood.

—Laura McKee
Biblical counseling chair, Christ for the Nations Institute

"*Welcome to parenting—where the mundane becomes pure joy!*" Those were the words inscribed by Carol in a parenting book she and Craig gave us when we were expecting our baby girl. Carol's words and perspective in my early years of parenting were far more impactful than the expert parenting book she shared. I'm so glad she's now written a book so that countless families can be influenced and blessed as ours has been. Her youngest child was a 3-year-old when our daughter was born so Carol was ahead of me and her example, as well as her words, profoundly affected our intentionality and vision in parenting. She and Craig were wonderful shepherds for my husband and me as new parents and their influence remains 25 years later.

As I read Carol's words in this book, I'm struck by how different the tone is from most *mommy posts* I see on social media and I know that her voice is needed for this generation. I'm reminded of Fred Rogers, who impacted children's television for generations and whose wisdom, calm, and intentionality in relating to children ran counter to the other children's programming of the time but has now been recognized as especially significant and wise. I believe the same can be said for Carol McLeod's wisdom in her guidance and encouragement for mothers in today's culture.

If you open your heart to the wise perspective shared here, I believe you will grow more joyful, more resilient in hardship and disappointment, more patient, gracious, and intentional, and will arrive at the front porch of seeing your child off into the world with greater hope and fewer regrets. I'm thankful that when I look at our adult daughter, I can still see the benefits of Carol's influence.

—Marilyn Freebersyser
Pastor's wife

As a woman, I can confirm that the beginning of every day, there needs to be a conscious choice to set my eyes on Jesus, choose joy, and find at least three things in my day for which I can express gratitude. Biblical instruction, especially from woman who have gone before me in experiences and life, is essential to build on that foundation of daily necessity. Carol McLeod is at the top of my list when seeking godly discipline and instruction. My time in life has brought me to the role of mother and as I've always believed and expressed to others, it takes a tribe to raise kids and do life as a kingdom-seeking/living family. After reading and working through *Rooms of a Woman's Heart*, I can only encourage other mamas and mamas-to-be to find inspiration, encouragement, and instruction from this book. Not only does this work of godly art encourage you in motherhood, but it also gives perspective of how God views us as His children! Each room is a direct correlation to the direction God desires for us in identity and purpose. Not to mention bringing joy to motherhood that is not always a place of joy!

—*Jillian Rae Merriam*
Cohort leader, MOPS (Mothers of Preschoolers)
HR manager

Rooms of a
Mother's
HEART

A Sacred Call and an Eternal Purpose

CAROL M^CLEOD

WHITAKER
HOUSE

ROOMS OF A MOTHER'S HEART
A Sacred Call and an Eternal Purpose

Carol McLeod Ministries
P.O. Box 1294
Orchard Park, NY 14127
855-569-5433
www.carolmcleodministries.com

ISBN: 978-1-64123-656-0 | eBook ISBN: 978-1-64123-657-7
Printed in the United States of America
© 2021 by Carol Burton McLeod

Whitaker House | 1030 Hunt Valley Circle | New Kensington, PA 15068
www.whitakerhouse.com

Library of Congress Cataloging-in-Publication Data
Names: McLeod, Carol Burton, 1954– author.
Title: Rooms of a mother's heart : a sacred call and an eternal purpose / Carol McLeod.
Description: New Kensington, PA : Whitaker House, 2021. | Summary: "Using the analogy that a woman's heart is a home, author shares personal and biblical accounts with the goal of encouraging young women to embrace the calling of motherhood and older mothers to look back fondly on the trials and triumphs of raising their children"— Provided by publisher.
Identifiers: LCCN 2021005315 (print) | LCCN 2021005316 (ebook) | ISBN 9781641236560 (trade paperback) | ISBN 9781641236577 (ebook)
Subjects: LCSH: Motherhood--Religious aspects—Christianity. | Home—Religious aspects--Christianity.
Classification: LCC BV4529.18 .M376 2021 (print) | LCC BV4529.18 (ebook) | DDC 248.8/431—dc23
LC record available at https://lccn.loc.gov/2021005315
LC ebook record available at https://lccn.loc.gov/2021005316

1 2 3 4 5 6 7 8 9 10 11 ꗑ 28 27 26 25 24 23 22 21

Dedication

Lovingly dedicated to
Carolyn Joy-Belle McLeod Barker

After three lively, rambunctious little boys…
there came a gift of pink!
Bows and ruffles, sweet songs, and little girl hugs.

We called you "Joy-Belle" from the beginning
and you have always lived up to your name.

When you were only eight years old,
you gave me a Christmas gift from the dollar store.
It was a small plate and on it were the words,

"A daughter is just a little girl who grows up to be your best friend!"

Those words are poignantly true for me.

And now…it is your turn.

It is your turn to mother a baby girl who is also a miracle.

I pray that she will open your heart to the wonder of motherhood
and that you, too, will know the delight of raising a daughter
who grows up to be your best friend.

You are always in my heart.

CONTENTS

Foreword.. 17

Acknowledgments 19

Introduction: An Invitation to the Heart of Motherhood 23

    1. Welcome Home 31

    2. The Birthing Room 39

    3. The Foundation 51

    4. The Nursery 65

    5. The Classroom 79

    6. A Pink Bedroom.. 93

    7. A Blue Bedroom 105

    8. The Corner 119

    9. The Library.. 137

    10. The Music Room 145

    11. The Family Room.. 155

    12. The Kitchen... 185

13. The Laundry Room 199

14. The Prayer Closet 211

15. The Front Porch 221

Appendix A: Books for Every Age and Stage 235

Appendix B: Recipes from the McLeod Kitchen 249

About the Author 256

FOREWORD

*M*other. It is impossible to hear that word without emotion. What do you feel, deep down, when you read the word *mother?*

And why does the word *mother* carry so much power to create emotion?

Whether we want to acknowledge it or not, our mother left us a legacy. For some of us, that legacy is unadulterated love; for others, the legacy is devastating heartbreak and loss. And for most of us, the legacy is a mixture of both belonging and pain. *Mother.* She is a powerful force that can launch us into life from a sturdy core of belonging and confidence, or from a hollow shell as an emotional nomad.

Whatever the legacy, we carry it forward, and as we become mothers ourselves, we can feel a shadow. The shadow can be a fear that we will not live up to our benevolent and wise mothers, or it can be the haunting of wounds from the past that echo in the deepest rooms of our aching hearts.

Then comes this book by our beloved Carol McLeod and we are suddenly not alone. Respectfully yet intimately, Carol holds our hand and takes us through every room of our own mother's heart. She is with us in each room, helping us to grow comfortable and skillful in each area, as we no longer are alone to explore the vast and difficult-to-navigate terrain. And she reveals our precious Savior in each room.

Carol knows, as do we, that much is at stake, for we are talking about mothering the inner makings of our children. Carol mentors us, encourages us, holds us, challenges us, and...mothers us, from the wisdom-geyser of her older and wiser Jesus-filled mother's heart.

As a licensed psychologist and childhood trauma specialist, I was thrilled that Carol wrote this practical, well-rounded book on Christian parenting. Rather than being just a how-to guide, this book is written from the heart, as story after story reveals applicable truth that is smooth going down. You will laugh and tear up as you visit all the rooms in your mother's heart. Your questions, even the ones you were afraid to ask, or did not know to ask, will be answered with tender yet profound wisdom. You will gain great courage in your mothering—and godly mothering does require heaps of courage, as you train your child in God's (sometimes counterculture) ways.

I look forward to your heart finding the mentoring, encouragement, wisdom, and strength you need as you push forward in your motherhood, finding skillfulness and fullness in all the rooms of your mother's heart. Moreover, I look forward to your children, who will be filled with positive emotion one day when they read the word *mother*, as they will have absorbed all you have invested in the core of who they are.

—*Barbara Lowe, PhD, LP, BCC, SEP*
Licensed Psychologist; Board Certified Coach
Somatic Experience Practitioner

ACKNOWLEDGMENTS

It is no small thing to say, "Thank you." Those two simple words just may be the most important words that a person ever utters.

When I was just a little girl, I was taught by my mother to write thank-you notes for gifts received, for compliments given, for meals served, and for acts of consideration. I could barely write my own name when she wrote the words, "Thank You," on the blackboard that graced the wall behind our kitchen table; I was expected to copy those words, say those words, and write those words.

My first thank-you notes were colorful pictures of rainbows, bunny rabbits, flowers, and little girls dancing under an umbrella. As the years passed and my vocabulary grew, the manner in which I sincerely thanked the people in life grew richer in content as well.

This, then, is my heartfelt thank-you note to the people in my life who have loved me, believed in me, and supported the message that you will find written between the covers of this book.

Thank you, Craig, for choosing me, for serving the Lord wholeheartedly, and for so much kindness that I never have felt that I deserved. Thank you for being a shepherd, a coach, and now a friend to our children. I am deeply grateful for you.

Thank you, Matthew, for forgiving me for all of my first-time mama mistakes and for loving me still. Your strength, wisdom, and excellence never cease to amaze me. You are my son and my friend. You are always in my heart. I am profoundly thankful for you.

Thank you, Christopher, for the gift of song that you have always provided for our family. Your music has healing power in its timbre and joy as its motivation. Whether you live near or far, you are always in my heart. I am infinitely grateful for you.

Thank you, Jordan, for your prayers, for your support, and for your cheerfulness. I don't just love you...but I also like you! You are our miracle child! God knew how much He needed you at this moment in history. Live for Him always. You are always in my heart I am beyond thankful for you.

Thank you, Joy, for always living up to your name and for lavishing the delight that is uniquely yours on everyone whom you meet. I can't wait to watch you mother your brood of little Barkers! You are always in my heart. I am completely grateful for you.

Thank you, Joni, for the years of sweet camaraderie that we shared as you were growing up. Those were some of the very favorite days of my entire life. Know that I am your mom—and nothing will ever change that! You are loved completely. You are always in my heart. I am so thankful for you.

Thank you, Emily, for the vitality and strength you have brought to our family after marrying Matthew, our firstborn son. How brave you were to enter this family filled with opinions, creativity, and strong wills! You have been a delight to us all and I am grateful that you are my daughter-in-love.

Thank you, Allie, for choosing Jordan and for loving us all unconditionally. Your prayers have already moved mountains and your heart for worship is pure and brave. Know that I am beyond grateful to call you my daughter-in-love and my friend.

Thank you, Chris, for loving Joy and for being a man of faith and wisdom. You are the answer to our prayers and we are in awe of what God is doing in you and through you. Thank you for shepherding your family, for working and studying diligently, and for your sweet stability. I am grateful that you are my son-in-love.

And then, to Olivia, Ian, Wesley, Amelia, Boyce, Elizabeth Joy, Jack, and the two little girls who are on their way—you are the ones who will carry the torch of family and faith to the next generation. Learn well, listen intently, watch carefully, and obey willingly. God has greatness hidden inside each one of you! And always remember that it pays to serve Jesus.

Thank you, Mom and Leo, for your prayers, your faith, and your encouragement. I ache to be with you but I know that the Lord is faithful in His care of you. I will always be *your girl*.

Thank you, Nanny, for your example of godly living and persistent prayer!

Thank you to my dad, Norman Burton, who made heaven his home nearly twenty years ago. I wouldn't be the woman I am today without your leadership and example. All the credit goes to you and all the glory goes to God!

Thank you to my dear friend and coworker, Angela Storm. You are a gift to me and to this ministry. Thank you for your labor of love, for your attention to details, for your prayer support, and for your faith. I love serving God with you!

Thank you to my friend and fellow warrior, Christy Christopher. You are making a difference, Christy. Never doubt the assignment on your life or the power that you have been given! I love *making hell smaller and heaven bigger* with you!

Thank you to the entire staff of Carol McLeod Ministries: Angela Storm, Danielle Stoltz, Linda Zielinski, Kirsten Monroe, Caleb Wiley, Kim Worden, and Christy Christopher. It is an undeserved honor to work with all of you as we endeavor to take the joy of His presence to this generation. You are appreciated, loved, and prayed for daily.

I must give a deep and sincere thank you to the Carol McLeod Ministries Board of Directors: Angela Storm, Kim Pickard Dudley, Sue Hilchey, Shannon Maitre, Tim Harner, Taci Darnelle, and Suzanne Kuhn. You are all the foundation of everything that we do. Thanks for being rock solid! Your wisdom, expertise, and personal support are invaluable.

It is my deep honor to give a rich and heartfelt thank you to the entire staff at Whitaker House, but especially to Bob Whitaker, Christine Whitaker, Peg Fallon, and Becky Speer. Your enthusiastic support, unmatched diligence, and wonderful friendship have filled my heart with new energy and enthusiasm. I am so blessed to be a Whitaker House author.

Thank you, John Mason and Suzanne Kuhn, for opening doors in the publishing industry for me. I am honored to call each of you my friend.

Thank you, Johnnie Hampton, for dreaming with me and for believing in the message of this ministry. Your professional and personal support means the world to me.

Thank you, Chris Busch, for your quiet and steady guidance. Your friendship is a true gift.

Thank you, Warrior Moms. What an honor it has been to fight battles with you! We are standing in strong faith that with God nothing is impossible. Thank you for holding up my arms in the battle.

Thank you also to the group of women who answer the desperate e-mails that come into Carol McLeod Ministries: Linda Hoeflich, Debby Summers, Angela Storm, Carolyn Hogan, Diane Phelps, Jill Janus, Shannon Maitre, Susie Hilchey, Keri Spring, Beth Nash, Debby Edwards, Linda Zielinski, Suzanne Adorian, and Christy Christopher. God is using you in mighty and dramatic ways! I am honored to partner with you in prayer and in encouragement.

Thank you to a magnificent team of friends who fill my life with encouragement and joy: Carolyn Hogan, Lisa Keller, Jill Janus, Dawn Frink, Debby Edwards, Diane Phelps, Brenda Mutton, Elaine Wheatley, Becky Harling, Melissa Thompson, Marilynda Lynch, Joy Knox, Sue Hilchey, Kim Pickard Dudley, Shannon Maitre, and Christy Christopher. Each one of you is a priceless gift from a loving and gracious Father.

And to Jesus, my Lord and Savior, thank You for calling me, equipping me, anointing me, and choosing me for Your grand purposes. I live to make hell smaller and heaven bigger! I live to honor You with every breath, with every word, and with every minute of my life! Thank You, Father, for allowing me the earthly delight of motherhood. All of the joy that I need is found in You!

INTRODUCTION

An Invitation to the Heart of Motherhood

Children are God's love-gift; they are heaven's generous reward. Children born to a young couple will one day rise to protect and provide for their parents. Happy will be the couple who has many of them! A household full of children will not bring shame on your name but victory when you face your enemies, for your offspring will have influence and honor to prevail on your behalf!

—Psalm 127:3–5 TPT

You are about to enter, or perhaps have already entered, the breathtaking, fulfilling, and frustrating address where motherhood lives. This residence is unequaled by any other season or event in life. When you are gifted with your first baby, the Lord looks at you lovingly and whispers, "I've prepared a place for you here! Welcome to the heart of motherhood!"

Once you step your foot across the threshold of this magnificent dwelling that is reserved for those who have been bestowed with the wonderful blessing of children, your life and your heart will never be the same.

Some of us arrived at this address after nine months of aching backs, swollen feet, and heartburn that culminated in giving birth to the visual demonstration of love. Others have tentatively knocked on the door of motherhood after long years of waiting for a baby to be delivered to their heart and their home through the miracle of adoption. Others, as foster moms, are wondering how long their stay will be at this significant address. However you arrived, know that God is the One who guided you here by His divine and loving wisdom.

HOWEVER YOU ARRIVED AT MOTHERHOOD, GOD IS THE ONE WHO GUIDED YOU HERE BY HIS DIVINE AND LOVING WISDOM.

We all long to be perfect moms—but that is not going to happen, dear one. *Perfect* is not a feasible option for any of us, but perhaps a better goal is *wonderful.*

This book is filled with stories, wisdom, tears, truth, lists, advice, and laughter. You might also discover the mother that you were meant to be within these pages.

At your initiation into the sweet yet noble world of motherhood, you quickly realize that your heart is never the same. Your heart grows exponentially when you become a mom and with that maternal growth, a new woman is established. You will discover a redesigned and much-improved version of the life that you formerly lived. Remember when you were allowed to sleep all night, when you fit into skinny jeans, and when your home was perpetually neat and orderly? You will love the *new* you so much more than the *old* you!

Your heart has now become a sumptuous home of the priceless treasury of motherhood. The repurposing of your heart may not be easy, but it will certainly fit you for the journey that you are on for the rest of your life. My heart's prayer for you is that you will not be a perfect mom, but that you will discover all of the ways that you can be a wonderful mom!

If your children have now flown the nest, consider this book as my invitation to once again sweetly stroll through the rooms of your heart and find new joy in the trials and triumphs of motherhood. You will laugh and you may cry, but you will also rediscover all of the ways that responding to God's highest calling has made you a better woman.

A Bold Young Woman

There once was a bold young woman who was filled with the assurance that no one had ever loved their children as much as she loved hers. This audacious yet dedicated thirty-something gal believed with every cell of her being that she was a particularly outstanding mother due to unconditional love, purposeful commitment, and grand creativity. Who wouldn't want her advice on motherhood?

Let's call this confident mother, *Carol*.

Carol had also always wanted to be an author, so she developed a sparkling book proposal. Somehow, by the hand of God, she garnered a personal interview with one of the top acquisitions editors in Christian publishing. She rarely left her five children, but felt that this opportunity was a divine appointment. So in true Carol fashion, she prepared two days' worth of meals, left a long list of instructions for her nervous husband, and kissed the dear, little faces goodbye.

For the first time in years, Carol wore an outfit that didn't smell of baby spit-up and no toddler clung to her legs. She boarded a plane that took her to Nashville, the Christian publishing mecca of the Western world, and bravely took the elevator to one of the top floors of the prestigious address.

The interview room was filled with the most respected men and women on the editorial and marketing staffs of this well-known publishing conglomerate. The secretary had made a copy of Carol's book proposal for everyone in the room and they were studying it as Carol's name was announced and she walked into that powerful atmosphere.

Carol was introduced to the people in whose hands her publishing fate was held (or so she thought) and she desired to come across as intelligent, thoughtful, and not too perky.

The man who was obviously in charge of the meeting sat behind a large desk. His walls were covered with diplomas, industry awards, family pictures, and Scripture verses. The room was large and warm but the atmosphere was cool and professional. When this man, who was respected from California to New York, finished reading Carol's proposal, he took off his glasses, looked into Carol's blue intrepid eyes, and smiled at her. He invited Carol to tell the committee about herself, her passions in life, and her past experience.

Carol meekly complied and felt that the interview was going exceptionally well. After about ten minutes of conversation, the man behind the desk thoughtfully rested his nose upon his tented fingers. He looked into the distance, pulled out his Bible, and turned to the apostle Paul's letter to Titus. He kindly said, "Carol, would you read Titus chapter two, verses three through five, to us?"

Carol quietly cleared her throat and humbly read the lovely admonition of Scripture so the entire room of important people could hear.

Older women likewise are to be reverent in their behavior, not malicious gossips nor enslaved to much wine, teaching what is good, so that they may encourage the young women to love their husbands, to love their children, to be sensible, pure, workers at home, kind, being subject to their own husbands, so that the word of God will not be dishonored. —Titus 2:3–5

Then, this giant in the great world of the publishing industry posed a simple question to the enthusiastic young mother: "Carol, who is supposed to teach the younger women to love their husbands, to love their children, and to be keepers of the home?"

Her voice wavered between wonder and regret as she respectfully replied, "The older women."

He gazed at her with love and encouragement in his eyes. "Carol," he said, "someday you will write a book on motherhood…but today is not that day. Go home and raise your children for the unshakable kingdom of Christ and when the time is right, you will write your book. I would be honored to publish it for you."

You have probably guessed by now that the very young and ambitious Carol has humbly transformed into the older and wiser Carol whose words you are reading today.

That publishing sage is now in heaven and although I have felt his consummate belief in me through the years, he is not the one who is publishing my book on motherhood. He did, however, give me the wisdom that I needed as a young, driven mother.

Today is the "someday" that I longed for three decades ago when I thought that I was the world's expert on motherhood. What I realize today is that there is no such thing as an expert on motherhood; there are simply women who have chosen to give their hearts and souls to the highest calling in the world. I am one of those women.

THERE ARE NO EXPERTS ON MOTHERHOOD, ONLY WOMEN WHO HAVE CHOSEN TO GIVE THEIR HEARTS AND SOULS TO THE HIGHEST CALLING IN THE WORLD.

When You Are Young

I want to speak with extreme gentleness as I woo you into reading this book; I don't want to come across as cocky or as a know-it-all. But let me just say this to the young moms: when you are young and raising your family, you are certain that you have all of the answers.

When you are young...

- You know that if you serve a diet of healthy meals, you will give your children the opportunity to become healthy adults.

- You understand that if you discipline fairly yet lovingly, you will not injure their souls.

- You believe that if you limit screen time, they will likely develop wholesome interests such as music, reading, and science.

- You know that if you choose to homeschool, send them to a Christian school, or be very involved in the public school, they will grow into moral adults.

- You declare that if you take them to Sunday school every week, have family devotions, or require Bible memorization, surely your brood of progeny will choose Christ in the long haul of their lives.

Most of all, you know that children need parents and your children are stuck with you.

Isn't it true that nothing is ever as predictable as we believe it to be when we are naively and enthusiastically young? I don't want to discourage any of the young moms who are discipling and parenting their children with excellence and zeal. I will be your loudest cheerleader, your biggest fan, and your most passionate intercessor!

However, young moms, I will tell you this: you need an older mom or two in your life. You need someone who has lived through sleepless nights, strong-willed two-year-olds, science projects, middle school emotions, high school angst, and college stress to add equilibrium to your enthusiasm and ardor. You need someone who has raised a quiverful of children from whom you can garner wisdom when the nights are short and the days are long. You need someone in your life who has not lost her joy as her children have left the safe nest of the home.

 YOUNG MOMS NEED AN OLDER MOM OR TWO IN THEIR LIVES WHO CAN SERVE AS THE VOICE OF EXPERIENCE.

There is a powerful and unavoidable reason why the Bible sets the framework for older mothers to encourage and teach younger mothers. I believe it is because we all need the voice of experience in our lives rather than the opinions of peers or novices. You don't just need a friend; you need an expert.

What Is Your Goal in Motherhood?

If your goal was to play the grand piano on the massive stage at Carnegie Hall, you probably wouldn't take piano lessons from someone who only knew how to play "Chopsticks," even if they played that simple melody extremely well.

If your life dream was to be a well-known chef at a five-star restaurant, you likely would not remain under the tutelage of someone whose go-to lunch for her children was canned tomato soup and saltine crackers, no matter how heartily they ate it.

If you were training for a marathon, it would be foolish to hire a trainer who had only walked once around the block.

There is a sobering story in the first book of Kings that serves as a reminder of the importance of listening to those who are older than you are. Solomon's son Rehoboam had taken his father's place as the king of Israel. The young king consulted with the elders who had served his father honorably, but he refused their advice and wisdom. Then, Rehoboam consulted with the young men with whom he had grown up. He listened solely to their novice counsel and during his reign, Israel was continually at war. I wonder what would have happened if Rehoboam had submitted himself to the wise counsel of men with leadership experience.

Do you understand my loving point? If you sincerely desire to raise healthy, productive, moral, and emotionally sound children all the way to adulthood, then you just might need to listen to a mom who has raised not perfect children but certainly productive young adults. You need a mom who is realistic, not just idealistic, about what it requires to raise a young man or a young woman who is filled with faith.

YOU NEED A MOM WHO IS REALISTIC ABOUT WHAT IT REQUIRES TO RAISE A YOUNG MAN OR A YOUNG WOMAN WHO IS FILLED WITH FAITH.

And, at times, you just might need to listen to a mom with some battle scars!

I would love to be that older mom in your life. I have sent five babies to heaven and have had the honor and privilege of raising five incredible children to adulthood. I am the mother-in-law to two amazing daughters-in-law and one brilliant son-in-law. But the most engaging aspect of my life currently is that I am now "Marmee" to eight wonders of the world, with two more baby girls on the way.

Although you might not always agree with my perspective, I hope that you will prayerfully consider my experience and honor my prudence in the splendid field of motherhood.

One Thousand Lives

Many years ago, I read the story of a young woman from the heart of Texas who had responded to the call to preach the gospel of Christ to the people of Korea. Ruby Kendrick was only twenty-four years old when she dedicated herself to teaching, praying for, and taking care of sick children in Songdo, Korea. Ruby was young and beautiful; she could have accomplished many impressive achievements had she chosen to live her life in the comfort of America. However, she chose to give her life for a generation of Korean children.

Ruby died from fatigue just eight months after setting foot on her beloved soil of Korea. Her untimely death inspired other Americans to take her place.

Ruby's is only one of 570 graves in the Foreigners' Cemetery Park in Seoul, South Korea, that honors Christian martyrs. On Ruby's tombstone are engraved these fierce yet gentle words:

If I had a thousand lives to live Korea should have them all.

My heart lies in puddles as I contemplate who this woman was, the price that she paid, and how deeply she loved the little ones on foreign soil.

I feel the same way about motherhood and I hope that by the closing page of this book, you will feel the same way, too. Perhaps the inscription on my tombstone and on yours someday will read, "If I had a thousand lives to live, motherhood would have them all."

The most important work you will ever do will be within the walls of your own home. —Harold B. Lee

1

Welcome Home!

*By wisdom a house is built, and by understanding it is established;
and by knowledge the rooms are filled with all precious and pleasant
riches.* —Proverbs 24:3–4

Welcome, my friend! Welcome to my home and to my heart. Welcome to
my years of mothering a brood of children so different, so complex, and yet so
wonderful that even now, my heart aches over the opportunity that the Father
Himself gave to me. As I look back upon my years of hands-on mothering
from my current vantage point of life, I wish that I could do it again…and
again…and again.

My deep desire to live once more in the trenches of motherhood has nothing to do with regrets but everything to do with the joy and purpose that are
only richly mined in the days of motherhood. I will be the first to assure you
that I was not a perfect mom; some days, I think that perhaps there was more
for which I needed to be forgiven than applauded. However, in all of my years
of motherhood, I truly unlocked my destiny. I discovered unmatched purpose
and I found intimacy with Christ.

A Treasury of Strength

For thousands of years and in a myriad of cultures, women have forged identity, unconditional love, and vast purpose in the calling of motherhood. From Eve to Sarah to Leah to Hannah to Ruth to Elizabeth to Mary, the Scriptures are filled with the stories of the heart of a woman who was given the divine opportunity to raise the next generation by a call of the Father. When I get to heaven, I can't wait to sit down with all of the mothers who went before me and ask them the questions that every mother desires to ask:

- How did you milk the goats, manage a clean tent, and keep a toddler away from scorpions in the desert?

- Was it hard to make sure that young David stayed away from lions and tigers and bears? Oh, my!

- What did you do when Abraham took Isaac up the mountain? What were you feeling in that moment?

- Were you embarrassed when John chose to wear camel hair and eat locusts as a teenager?

However, the heart that I most desire to inspect is the heart of Mary, the mother of Jesus Christ.

But Mary treasured all these things, pondering them in her heart.
—Luke 2:19

Inside the soul of every mother lies a heart that becomes a repository of sweet memories, hard lessons, glorious victories, ordinary days, glaring failures, and God's grace over the years of mothering. The heart of a mother becomes home to jokes around the dinner table, holiday traditions, the tears of childhood, and the love that only a mother knows.

THE HEART OF A MOTHER BECOMES HOME TO JOKES AROUND THE DINNER TABLE, HOLIDAY TRADITIONS, THE TEARS OF CHILDHOOD, AND THE LOVE THAT ONLY A MOTHER KNOWS.

This tender heart that has given birth to the future of mankind or has lovingly adopted the seeds of the next generation also develops rooms of unsurpassed greatness and quiet strength. These are the rooms that we will be examining on the pages of this book—the rooms of a mother's heart.

In every generation, mothers must answer the call to be what no one else can be for their children and do what no one else is able to do for their children. Mothers must accept the biblical call to motherhood, or we will be guilty of producing a generation who wanders in the wilderness of moral deficiency, racial division, and underdeveloped conscience. I am not suggesting that mothers are the cause of society's ills, nor are they mankind's saviors, but the future of our nation, our schools, our church, our neighborhoods, and our world depends largely upon what we do with the children under our care.

> A mother is she who can take the place of all others but whose place no one else can take.　　—Cardinal Gaspard Mermillod

Is there a calling that is more significant or more glorifying to God than motherhood? I think not!

We live in a society and culture in which the call to motherhood is denigrated or scoffed at. We are told that a woman loses her identity in motherhood and that the years spent wiping noses, changing diapers, and reading books are the wasted years of a woman's life. My friend, nothing could be farther from the truth than those words of cultural deception. I believe that it is possible to actually find yourself in motherhood, to discover talents and strengths that you have never before tapped into during the rich and beautiful season of being called "Mommy" by a tribe of little people.

 IF YOU WANT TO CHANGE THE WORLD, THEN DECIDE THAT YOU WILL PASSIONATELY MOTHER THE ONES YOU HAVE BEEN GIVEN TO RAISE.

I also fiercely believe that it is possible to make a long-lasting impact on the world when you give yourself to training the children under your watch. If you want to change the world, then decide that you will passionately mother the ones you have been given to raise. Money does not equal significance and promotions do not communicate value. It is in dying to self that we become significant in the kingdom of our Creator and it is in serving others that we achieve true greatness. The Word's way has never been the world's way.

Let me hasten to say that I realize that women must often work outside the home in order to pay the bills, save for college, and feed their children. I understand and I realize that motherhood requires great adjustment and challenges. What I deeply desire that you understand as you read the pages of this book is that motherhood is the highest calling a woman embraces; it is not an inevitable frustration added in to an already busy life.

When a woman works outside the home, it is not a betrayal of motherhood, nor is it an alliance with the culture. It is often a serious necessity. Please be kind to yourself as a mother and as a woman whether you are able to stay home, work part-time, or work full-time. The chief principle should be to give your whole heart to your children in the times that you are together. This is a foundational aspect of motherhood.

Home is the nicest word there is.   —Laura Ingalls Wilder

Complete Joy

When you truly understand the deep purpose of motherhood, the joy will come rushing into your home and into your heart. If you falsely believe that you are merely a babysitter, a cook, a maid, or a laundress, there will be little joy in your area of influence. However, if you are finally able to convince yourself that you are changing the course of history for the kingdom of God, it is in that miraculous moment that the lavish joy of motherhood will come rushing into your life in magnificent proportions.

Joy always follows knowing one's purpose. You, as a mother, are a woman of eternal and perpetual purpose! History would not be complete without the lives of the little ones whose diapers you are changing today. There would be a vacuum in the course of humanity without the talents and creativity of the children who are finger painting at your kitchen table today.

You are raising the Daniels, the Esthers, and the Peters of the next generation, so do it with unbridled joy! The most expansive work you will ever complete will be among the ordinary people whom you know the best and love the most.

All of heaven is roaring in approval at the joy that you are cultivating in motherhood!

And this is what I can guarantee you: for every long night, God gives His own strength to weary mothers who simply ask for it. For every early and daunting morning, He delivers His faithfulness to mothers who spend time with Him. Cry if you must, knowing that even your tears are precious to Him and not one of them goes unnoticed in the throne room of God.

Every prayer you have prayed has been heard, sweet mama. He has inclined His very ear over the gates of heaven and has given you His undivided attention. Every desire you have whispered to your heavenly Father is not forgotten. Your desires are of utmost importance to Him. He longs to hear you express your heartfelt desires and then lay them at His nail-scarred feet.

Every song you choose to sing in the middle of piles of Legos, macaroni and cheese stuck to the kitchen cabinet, and little ones clinging to your legs is a glorious anthem to heaven's ears. God smiles when a mother sings!

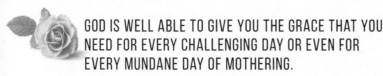

GOD IS WELL ABLE TO GIVE YOU THE GRACE THAT YOU NEED FOR EVERY CHALLENGING DAY OR EVEN FOR EVERY MUNDANE DAY OF MOTHERING.

God is well able to give you the grace that you need for every challenging day or even for every mundane day of mothering. He loves your children so much more than you ever could and He has chosen to partner with you in developing their character, their temperament, and their walk of faith. Your greatest accomplishment this side of heaven may have little to do with your college degree, the level of income that you accrue, or the awards that you garner. Your greatest accomplishment in life will inevitably be someone whom you have raised.

You have been chosen to raise the specific children in your home—I dare you to do it with grace, with strength, with honor, and with joy!

You are enough, dear mother. You are more than enough because you have the Father.

Inspection Day

Over the course of more than forty years of marriage, my husband Craig and I have bought many homes and have learned the importance of a pre-purchase home inspection if we wish to live in a house with as little frustration as possible. We have lived in small homes and large ones, old houses that were woefully outdated and new homes with the most up-to-date amenities. We have lived in country homes and university apartments; we have resided in small towns and in the suburbs of large cities. Our hard-learned lesson in acquiring a place in which to live is that we should never move into the residence without first having an inspection take place.

Craig and I were living in a home that was much too small for our family of five children and one dog. We didn't have the financial resources to buy a bigger home, so we simply began to pray about our options. One day, a very successful man in our town contacted us to let us know that his family home was on the market. He wondered if we would be interested in looking at this three-story Williamsburg home set on four acres in a park-like setting. He and Craig had been high school friends and he was willing to offer us a wonderful price on this absolutely gorgeous piece of real estate.

I fell in love with the home the instant I walked through the front door. I actually began to weep because it was hard for me to believe that we could actually live in a home so beautiful and so accommodating to our needs. Over the next forty-eight hours, Craig and this generous man agreed on a price that was well below what the home was actually worth. However, the owner's one request was that we forego the inspection. Of course, we agreed. We would never be able to afford a home such as this one without this man's benevolence, so we moved toward closing with a handshake and a smile.

As much as we appreciated the buying terms, we quickly learned that we should have had an inspection. The windows leaked and the plumbing was in need of some serious repairs. The roof had to be replaced and repeated moisture had warped the sunroom floor.

Yet we loved the home and continued to build a rich family life there. However, we also learned a difficult lesson: before you buy a home, you must have an inspection.

Will you join me in this fascinating inspection of the rooms of a mother's heart? Will you help me ascertain what is strong and vital in the heart that is mothering the little lives you have been given? Will you gently allow the Holy Spirit to make needed repairs and update your habits and attitudes? Will you, perhaps, invite the Lord to renovate the entire heart that is home to your world of motherhood?

My heart's desire and deepest prayer for you as a woman in the trenches of motherhood is that you will find Jesus and joy in every room of your heart. I pray that your life will be saturated with both direction and determination as never before. I hope that you will begin to plant the vibrant flowers of peace, kindness, and faithfulness around the exterior of your heart and clear away the dust bunnies of frustration that our culture may have created.

Most of all, I am confident that as we inspect the rooms of your heart, you will enter a brand new day of motherhood. I believe that you will discover the woman that you were meant to be from the very beginning of time.

You can tell,
When you open the door!
You can tell,
If there's love in a home!

Every table and chair seems to smile,
Do come in, come and stay for a while.
You almost feel you've been there once before,
By the shine and glow of the room!

And the clock seems to chime,
Come again anytime,
You'll be welcome wherever you roam!
You can tell when there's love in a home![1]

---

1. Gene De Paul and Johnny Mercer, "Love in a Home," from the 1956 musical *L'il Abner*.

2

The Birthing Room

Let your father and your mother be glad, and let her rejoice who gave birth to you.   —Proverbs 23:25

On the day of a baby's birth, another birth is simultaneously taking place—for a mother is also born in that place of blood, pain, and fortitude. A woman who walks into the hospital great with child is a decidedly different woman who then walks out with a tiny baby in her arms. A woman who is bestowed with a miracle from another woman's womb becomes a distinct person in that heartbeat when *hers* instantly becomes *mine*.

In the birthing room, in the midst of productive pain, intense breathing, and unending minutes, a woman's heart is stretched to new possibilities and greater concerns.

After years of infertility and yearning desire, the heart of a mother is also born when she holds her adopted child for the first time.

The birthing room of a mother's heart is unlike any other room due to the miracles that take place in the process and in the journey. There is a miracle that is happening to you, dear mom, and it is happening in the birthing room of your heart.

Who Am I?!

I was raised in the 1960s and '70s at the height of a cultural period known as the women's movement. Women were breaking into careers that had historically belonged only to men. Women were running for the highest offices in the land, anchoring network news, and competing for jobs at NASA, on Wall Street, and as university presidents.

 MY MOM AND HER FRIENDS WORE APRONS AND COOKED FOUR-COURSE DINNERS EVERY NIGHT WHILE WEARING HIGH HEELS.

I was wedged between my mom and her friends—who wore aprons and cooked four-course dinners every night while wearing high heels—and the cataclysmic change that was taking place in America. My mother and her peers were known to preserve an entire winter's supply of vegetables in one week or less, make enough spaghetti sauce and zucchini bread from their kitchen garden to feed the entire state of Rhode Island, and wet mop the floor every morning by 7:00 a.m. The coffee pot was always warm in our home, clothes were always neatly folded and put away in alphabetical order by color, and a speck of dust was attacked with a fierce position of defiance. My mom ironed every day of the week—even undershirts, pillowcases, and handkerchiefs. No wrinkles were allowed in our family home!

To my mother and her friends, success was being nominated for the presidency of the PTA or being asked to teach the women's Sunday school class. Prominence was defined as being asked to chair the annual turkey dinner at church.

I was sandwiched between the sweet, stable traditions that my mother, her mother, and her grandmother had basked in and the aggressive freedom of the women's movement. When Jane Fonda and Gloria Steinem were burning their bras, I was being taught to write thank-you notes with perfect penmanship and wore white gloves to tea parties and church events.

As I grew into my teenage and young adult years, I realized that the winds of change were blowing across the culture. I felt trapped yet exhilarated, pulled yet pushed. I wondered what type of world would be my reality as I stepped onto the threshold of womanhood.

I started college in the mid-1970s with grand anticipation! I knew that it was in the next four years that I would discern God's specific will for my life as a person and as a woman. I wondered if I would marry a pastor or become a network news anchor. Would I teach third grade in my local school district or would I become a Pulitzer Prize-winning author?

I WAS SANDWICHED BETWEEN THE SWEET, STABLE TRADITIONS OF MY MOTHER AND THE AGGRESSIVE FREEDOM OF THE WOMEN'S MOVEMENT.

I had dreams and plans for my life, but I was unsure if these were the growth shoots of seeds planted by my culture, my family, or my faith. I longed for my destiny to match the one that God had crafted specifically for me since the beginning of all time.

The motto of the university I attended was, "Make no little plans here," and I intended to comply. I wanted to be the one university student whose plans were the biggest and grandest. Our callings and destinies were discussed at every late night study session, every cafeteria meal, and every prayer meeting on campus. As a student body, we were encouraged to, "Hear My voice, to go where My light is dim, where my voice is heard small...even to the uttermost bounds of the earth." I accepted the challenge with my whole heart!

Every day on this unique campus, filled with a dynamic group of students from around the world, I was rubbing shoulders with girls who wanted to be the first woman to step foot on the moon, the first woman Supreme Court justice, or even had the moxie to believe that she could be the first woman president of America! Imagine that!

As I drank it all in, eavesdropped on every conversation, and sat in rapt attention at every chapel, I made a determination for my life. I decided that whatever I did, whether it was large or small in the eyes of the world, I would never settle for mediocrity in my life. I partnered with the One who created me and asked that He would require me, as His daughter, to stand on my tiptoes every day of my life. I still wasn't sure of the *what* but I knew the *how*. Whatever I did with my life, I would tackle it with rare enthusiasm and heartfelt passion.

In the second semester of my senior year in college, I met a young man whose faith and passion for Christ amazed me. Before the evening was over, I asked God, "Lord, is Craig McLeod my destiny?"

We were married six months later.

We spent the first two years of our married life on staff at the university from which we had recently graduated. We then moved to the Deep South, where Craig was on staff at church as an associate pastor. I began to work for a national scholarship organization for young women and in true *Carol* style, I had dreams of leading the organization someday. How presumptuous of me!

I discovered that I loved the corporate world and felt that I could make a difference in the lives of thousands of young women. I found fulfillment in working with national sponsors and universities in their quest to discover the brightest and best of the next generation.

 I LOOKED OVER AT MY HANDSOME HUSBAND AND DRYLY ANNOUNCED, "JUST SO YOU KNOW, I DON'T WANT TO HAVE CHILDREN."

One afternoon as Craig and I were driving down a boulevard whose trees were dripping with decades of moss, I looked over at my handsome husband and dryly announced, "Just so you know, I don't want to have children. I have found my calling in life and I intend to give every ounce of talent and knowledge in me to making a difference in corporate America."

Craig didn't argue with me nor did he respond verbally; he just prayed.

Be Born in Me

I was tired and nauseous for weeks in the spring of 1980 and thought I had contracted a relentless strain of the flu. However, after finally going to the doctor, I learned that I was pregnant. I was going to be a mom!

In that instant, my heart began to turn toward home and something unfamiliar was being birthed in me. Like Mary, I began to ponder the changes in my heart and open myself up to something greater than my own desires or preferences.

On January 29, 1981, at 5:35 p.m., in the delivery room of the University of South Alabama Medical Center, I realized the purpose for which I had been born. I had been created to be a mother. I was born anew that day and everything in me that had been hibernating under the guise of culture and prominence suddenly came to life. The reason that I had been born in the heart of the Father was awakened within me; it was not a seed planted in me by my culture nor was it cultivated by the hopes and dreams of other people. The moment of Matthew's birth was an instant like no other—it was a single moment in time that would define and frame every other moment of my entire existence. I was a mom. I was born to be a mother.

As I looked at Matthew's exquisite little face and counted his ten tiny fingers and ten oh-so-cute toes, I realized that I was responsible for his very soul. I would be held accountable one day for the development of his gifts and talents. Craig and I would answer to the Lord for the manner in which we trained this little man who was so fresh from heaven. As an ordinary woman, I had been given the opportunity to nurture this life for use in the kingdom of God.

Feminists continued to burn their bras while I nursed my baby and sang over him. Other women climbed my recently vacated corporate ladder while I prayed over my baby and drank in the wonder of his existence.

OTHER WOMEN CLIMBED MY RECENTLY VACATED CORPORATE LADDER WHILE I PRAYED OVER MY BABY AND DRANK IN THE WONDER OF HIS EXISTENCE.

Even today, nearly four decades later, I believe that I have been born at this time in history to remind women of the eternal purpose and calling hidden in motherhood.

I will not keep silent. I adamantly refuse to extract my identity or my destiny from the culture's expectation of me.

I Am the Women's Movement!

When Queen Esther was called upon to make a monumental sacrifice in order to save a generation of people, this question was posed to her, *"Who knows whether you have come to the kingdom for such a time as this?"* (Esther 4:14 NKJV).

When Matthew was laid on my chest in that hospital birthing room, a world-changing woman was born. I received a download from heaven's assignment room when my firstborn son entered the world that has never left my heart. I knew that I had been called by the One who had created me to raise a generation of children who would change the course of history for Christ and His kingdom.

I realized shortly after Matthew's birth that *I* am the woman's movement! I will be used for a greater and more eternal purpose than this world could ever offer a woman. I might be called upon to swim upstream from my culture but I will rely on His strength to do it with joy.

OUR CULTURE MIGHT PROPOSE THAT YOU WILL ONLY BE A SIGNIFICANT WOMAN IF YOU EARN A HIGH SALARY, BUT GOD'S WAYS ARE HIGHER AND MORE ETERNAL.

Ever since that warm winter day on the Gulf Coast of Alabama in 1981, I have realized that perhaps the best part of one's destiny is that it is forged in private in the birthing room of God. Our culture might propose that you will only be a significant woman if you earn a high salary, achieve significant degrees, or obtain public recognition, but God's ways are higher and more eternal than the pitch of this world. God uses the backside of the desert to work in a woman's heart and gives her a child when all hope is gone. God presents Himself on the dusty streets of life and announces to a beloved daughter that a baby is a miracle. The Father meets a grieving, destitute woman in a field of grain and gives her a lasting legacy in that hidden place.

A Private Place

A birthing room is a private place where only intimate friends and medical experts are invited. It is of vital importance that you carefully select the team of family, friends, and mentors who are allowed into the birthing room of your heart. Others may try to barge in and give their opinion concerning your purpose and destiny in life, but maintain your perspective and only listen to those who have your best interests at heart and know you very well.

Any woman who has given birth physically knows that you lose all sense of modesty when you are in the birthing position. I know that this is true in an emotional sense for women who have adopted babies as well. The birthing process, whether experienced physically or by adoption, exposes everything that is within us to those around us. It is for this very reason that you must be careful who is invited into the place where you give birth to identity and calling.

If you are struggling to give birth to your true destiny and calling, invite those in who have discovered their eternal purpose in life. You might consider building relationships with older women who have stayed true to their mission in life without wavering and with joy.

It is always appropriate, in your quest for creating lifetime objectives, to call in the experts! A counselor or a pastor is often what is needed to help deliver peace into the delivery room of your heart so that you are able to confidently give birth to that for which you have been called.

The birthing room of your heart should be filled with those who love you and are cheering for you on your journey. I always encourage pregnant women to cease to listen to the horror stories of others and only fill their hearts with the positive testimonies of those who see the purpose in spite of the pain. So it is with you, my friend. As you endeavor to produce the destiny of God in your life, listen to those who will encourage you and hold your hand during the transition.

The power of finding beauty in the humblest things makes home happy and life lovely.　　　　　　　　　　　　—Louisa May Alcott

Ordinary Miracles

The birthing room of a woman's heart does not cease to exist the day that she walks out of the hospital with a new baby, a new identity, or a new reason for being. When you are a mother, there is always the possibility of an ordinary miracle coming to life in the midst of the mundane. The door of the birthing room is never permanently closed because new discoveries are being made daily in the life of a dedicated mother!

In the birthing room of my heart, I have often unlocked the formerly concealed joy of the simple things in life. I have happened upon the unmatched delight of the achingly yet hidden familiar during the years of hands-on mothering. Who knew that a gnat could be so bothersome or that a caterpillar could be so engaging? Who knew that a baby's chortle could instantly change the atmosphere in a home or that a rich conversation with a ten-year-old could hold such a wealth of wisdom? Who knew that a peanut butter and jelly sandwich, a glass of cold milk, and a book of jokes would bring sunshine to an otherwise dreary, rainy day? Who knew?

IN THE BIRTHING ROOM OF MY HEART, I HAVE OFTEN UNLOCKED THE FORMERLY CONCEALED JOY OF THE SIMPLE THINGS IN LIFE.

I never would have discovered the raucous fulfillment of the mooing of a cow except through the eyes and ears of a two-year-old. I never would have been privy to the wonder of the roaring ocean and the ecstasy of gathering seashells had I not accompanied a five-year-old to the beach. I never would have known the enchantment of the first snowfall of the winter had I not gone for a walk in the brisk air with an eight-year-old. Motherhood delivers the gratification of ordinary miracles in the deepest places of a woman's soul. It is in those moments of simple yet profound satisfaction that she partners with God in giving birth to the glory for which mankind was created.

The glory of God is man fully alive!   —St. Irenaeus

Perhaps what happens during the context of a normal day that has been redefined by the vitality of childhood is that the childhood of the mother has tenderly been renewed. Maybe it is in mothering that we are born again to all that is resonant and memorable of the child we once were. As we partner with the Lord in raising our children for Him, conceivably a miracle happens inside the adult heart of a mother and she becomes a child once again.

Jesus called a little one to his side and said to them, "Learn this well: Unless you dramatically change your way of thinking and become teachable, and learn about heaven's kingdom realm with the wide-eyed wonder of a child, you will never be able to enter in. Whoever continually humbles himself to become like this gentle child is the greatest one in heaven's kingdom realm. And if you tenderly care for this little one on my behalf, you are tenderly caring for me."

—Matthew 18:2–5 TPT

Learn how to giggle again and how to wish on a dandelion as you blow its fluff away. Splash in puddles with your little ones and capture fireflies on a summer night. Awaken the wonder of childhood as you catch snowflakes on your tongue and let a caterpillar crawl up your arm. You will discover that you were born to dance in the music of childhood while guided by the wisdom of adulthood.

The Birth of Significance

Motherhood also gives birth to the most tremendous work that you will ever realize this side of eternity. The greatest work you will ever accomplish will be within the walls of your own home. The most expansive work you will ever produce will be among the ordinary people whose hearts belong to you.

There is no doctoral degree in mothering, but if you can stay the course, you will have earned and will certainly deserve that advanced degree in parenting with the highest of honors!

There is no Olympic event for living through two-year-old tantrums, but if you can keep your sanity during those days, you will have won a gold medal, flowers, and a pedestal—and if motherhood had a national anthem, it would be played in your honor!

There is no lifetime achievement award given to women who raise healthy children but believe me, my friend, God notices your labor of love and is giving you a standing ovation! Oh, my sister in Christ, all of heaven is roaring in approval of your uncommon life!

Prominence and success in our culture will never define the woman that Christ has called me to be. However, simply embracing the call to motherhood passionately and enthusiastically has accomplished a dignified significance within my soul.

> SIMPLY EMBRACING THE CALL TO MOTHERHOOD PASSIONATELY AND ENTHUSIASTICALLY HAS ACCOMPLISHED A DIGNIFIED SIGNIFICANCE WITHIN MY SOUL.

If I were to become the first woman president of the United States of America, it would pale in comparison to the years that I spent raising the children who were given to me. If I were to win the Nobel Peace Prize for an honorable and incomparable exploit, motherhood would still be my finest accomplishment. If I were to be recognized with prestigious and recognizable awards for talent on the stage or screen, my greatest talent would still be discovered in rocking babies to sleep, soothing the fears of childhood, and creating wonder in the soul of a child.

Every tear you have shed is precious to Him and He saves each tear in heaven in the Motherhood Hall of Fame.

Every song you choose to sing, when you would rather complain or cry, is a glorious anthem to heaven's ears! God smiles when you sing in the middle of your days of motherhood. God loves a common mother who breaks into song when the dishes are piled high, when the laundry is piled higher, and when the baby has been up all night teething.

You, as an ordinary woman, have given birth to God's answer for the next generation. You, as a participant in the plan of God, have been bequeathed a unique child even if your body did not writhe in the pain of childbirth; your heart has ached with the wretched pain of waiting for God to give you a child in His own generous manner. The hands of the Great Physician, even now, are gently nurturing you in your pain and in your promise. He has met you in the birthing room of your heart.

When God wants a great work done in the world or a great wrong righted, He goes about it in a very unusual way. He doesn't stir up His earthquakes or send forth His thunderbolts. Instead, He has a helpless baby born, perhaps in a simple home and of some obscure mother. And then God puts the idea into the mother's heart, and she puts it into the baby's mind. And then God waits. The greatest forces in the world are not the earthquakes and the thunderbolts. The greatest forces in the world are babies.

—E. T. Sullivan

3

The Foundation

For no one can lay a foundation other than the one which is laid, which is Jesus Christ.   —1 Corinthians 3:11

As with any other building, the foundation of a home determines its capacity for both weight and height. It must be able to support the load of the house that's being built, taking into account the design, overall size, and building materials. Without a strong foundation, the homeowner is likely to face costly repairs in the future.

What you have the capacity to become, both as a woman and as a mother, depends upon the foundational issues of your faith. If you want your life to be supported by your chosen foundation, then you must spend time in establishing a stalwart one that will stand the test of time and withstand the storms of life.

I believe there are foundational truths that you must build your home upon. If these truths are neglected or overlooked, the cracks of impatience, anger, and bitterness may cause your family to be on shaky ground. However, if you focus on the necessary foundational truths and create a home that is built upon this bedrock, then when the storms of life come—and come they will—your home will remain steadfast in the face of insurmountable odds.

IF YOU FOCUS ON THE NECESSARY FOUNDATIONAL TRUTHS, THEN WHEN THE STORMS OF LIFE COME, YOUR HOME WILL REMAIN STEADFAST IN THE FACE OF INSURMOUNTABLE ODDS.

The Word

My dad was a quiet general of the faith; he didn't bark orders nor did he demand honor but he gently and serenely lived a life of uncompromising commitment to the Word of God. His name will never be listed in anyone's Hall of Fame nor will he ever be recognized as a prestigious man in the eyes of the world; however, his extraordinary attention to the eternal truth of Scripture will ricochet through generations of those who have been impacted by his unpretentious life.

Dad was an early riser due to his childhood and young adult years spent on a dairy farm. He was accustomed to getting up before the sun to milk the cows and gather the eggs.

As a father, he was known for getting up as early as 4:30 a.m. in order to read the Bible before he had to plow the driveway, fix our lunches for school, or weed the family garden. Often, when I heard my dad stirring in the kitchen, I would also smell the aroma of his instant coffee laced with milk. As a very small child, I would creep downstairs to snuggle into his lap while he read the greatest Book ever written. When I was old enough to read on my own, Dad wrote Bible verses on computer cards so that I could read a portion of what he was reading each morning.

Every Saturday evening, Dad wrote a new Scripture verse on the blackboard that hung on the wall behind the kitchen table. Throughout the week, we talked about the verse and committed it to memory. The verse was erased on Saturday afternoons and Dad would challenge his three children to recite it from memory at the dinner table. He didn't give prizes or rewards for memorizing Scripture but his smile and his quiet, "Well done," was all the reward that I needed.

A Bible that's falling apart usually belongs to someone who isn't.
—Charles Spurgeon

Your children need to know that there are some things in this world that never change; they need to have an understanding that although the culture may evolve, there is a constant in their lives upon which they can rely. The truth of Scripture is the most valuable commodity that a family can build a life upon. When the Bible is honored in a home, it does a miracle in the lives of each family member. *"For the word of God is living and active"* (Hebrews 4:12); it will enable a family of diverse personalities and opinions to find unity and peace.

WHEN THE BIBLE IS HONORED IN A HOME, IT DOES A MIRACLE IN THE LIVES OF EACH FAMILY MEMBER.

When you treasure the Word of God and encourage your children to memorize His truths, it will enable them to navigate the teenage years with purity and righteousness.

How can a young man keep his way pure? By keeping it according to Your word.   —Psalm 119:9

The Bible will bring peace to troubled minds and comfort to raging emotions.

My soul weeps because of grief; strengthen me according to Your word.   —Psalm 119:28

The greatest gift you can give to your children is the foundation that only the Bible supplies. I am not talking about *preaching* to your children; I am referring to the absolute necessity of treasuring the Bible every day in your family home.

Visit many good books but live in the Bible.

—Charles Spurgeon

When we brought our babies home from the hospital, I placed their miniature hands on my Bible and I told them, "This is the Bible. It's God's Word to us. We love the Bible."

When our children were toddlers, we lined up all of their stuffed animals and talked about Noah's ark and about the importance of obeying God.

We used goldfish crackers to reenact Jesus's feeding of the 5,000. To the children's delight and surprise, goldfish crackers would appear all around the room.

Craig and I firmly believed that children only needed a twofold theology until they were about ten years old: they needed to know that Jesus loved them unconditionally and enthusiastically; and they needed to know that the Bible says children are to obey their parents.

Our goal as parents was to stress the truth of Scripture, its unchanging nature, and its application to our daily lives.

We were careful to talk about the Bible both reverently and joyfully. Craig and I deeply desired for our children to know that no one has a better idea than God and that the abundant life is the best life!

Let the word of Christ richly dwell within you, with all wisdom teaching and admonishing one another with psalms, hymns, and spiritual songs, singing with thankfulness in your hearts to God.

—Colossians 3:16

Children learn what they live. If they see their dear mama reading her Bible, they too will know the value and the joy that is found on the sacred pages of Scripture. I have always known that I would be unable to leave my children a legacy of earthly treasures, but I was more than able to give them that which will never corrupt or grow old.

Love the LORD your God with all your heart and with all your soul and with all your strength. These commandments that I give you today are to be on your hearts. Impress them on your children. Talk about them when you sit at home and when you walk along the road, when you lie down and when you get up.

—Deuteronomy 6:5–7 NIV

Honoring, memorizing, and reading the Word of God is a foundational issue of family life.

Worship

Children love to sing and dance! They love a good shout and the ability to give honor to others. I believe that the happiest of homes is the one in which worship is loud, perpetual, and sincere.

YOU SHOULD SING THE GREAT HYMNS OF FAITH TO YOUR BABY EVEN WHEN YOUR PRECIOUS CHILD IS STILL IN YOUR WOMB.

The first song that your baby should hear you sing is, "Jesus Loves Me." You should sing the great hymns of faith to your baby even when your precious child is still in your womb. A familiar song to an infant's ears should be the song that flows from his or her mother's own heart.

When you are up all night with a colicky baby, turn it into a worship service and sing rather than moan or cry.

When a strong-willed two-year-old begins to throw a tantrum, quietly teach your little one, "It's time to sing. Let's sing together. What song would you like to sing?"

We loved to sing this doxology around the dinner table, even though some of us sang off-key:

Praise God, from Whom all blessings flow;
Praise Him, all creatures here below;
Praise Him above, ye heavenly Host;
Praise Father, Son, and Holy Ghost. Amen.

At bedtime, the family serenade was the "Taps" song:

Day is done, gone the sun,
From the lake, from the hills, from the sky;
All is well, safely rest, God is nigh.

A family can never rejoice too much—it's just not possible! Worship will bind your family together in a way that little else is able to do. As a family, it's more important to sing praises to the Lord than it is to play sports or games together. As a family, it is more restorative to worship around the piano than to spend time at the library. Worship serves as an invisible yet constant relational glue that will stand the test of time and differences in personality.

WHEN A FAMILY CHOOSES TO WORSHIP GOD, THEY ARE CHOOSING TO LIVE IN THE DIVINE PLACE OF GOD'S DESIGN.

Worship is also the awareness that God is present in the middle of our lives. We acknowledge Him and His grace when we sing; when a family chooses to worship God, they are choosing to live in the divine place of God's design. We were created to make much of God, not to make much of ourselves. Teaching children from an early age to keep their eyes and heart set on Jesus in worship truly is a precious part of family life.

I will bless the LᴀRD *at all times: His praise shall continually be in my mouth.* —Psalm 34:1

We recently held a combined celebration of Father's Day and my husband's sixty-fifth birthday at our daughter Joy-Belle's home. Words of encouragement and blessing were said over Craig by each son or daughter, including one who joined us by phone. We ended our time together by gathering around the piano and our son Jordan led us all in worship. It was a moment I will never forget. The grandchildren lifted their little hands in the air, Craig's mom had tears running down her wrinkled cheeks, and Craig wept for joy.

And all my life You have been faithful
And all my life You have been so, so good
With every breath that I am able
Oh, I will sing of the goodness of God[2]

Does your family have a theme song? If not, there's no better time than today to choose one. Select an anthem that will carry your family through storms and fires, a melody that will be a stirring reminder of the faithfulness of God. Take a song for your very own that makes much of the Lord whom you serve.

Teaching your family to worship the Lord together is a foundational issue of family life.

Forgiveness

A family is a group of sinners who are living under one roof. I have yet to meet a healthy family who didn't require the power of immediate and unconditional forgiveness.

Our own family needed to be reminded of the necessity of forgiveness on a daily basis—sometimes hourly!

Bearing with one another, and forgiving each other, whoever has a complaint against anyone; just as the Lord forgave you, so must you do also. —Colossians 3:13

It is inevitable that children will fuss at each other from time to time and frustrations will arise. Inevitably, one child will react in anger and another will respond in like manner. The first response every time should be forgiveness to one another. A family unit is where our spiritual walk is honed and matured. If your children don't forgive one another, then they will someday find it impossible to forgive their spouses or others who have wronged them. We practice forgiveness in the home so that when we are out in the world, we know how and when to forgive.

---

2. Bethel Music, "Goodness of God," on *Victory* (Bethel Music, 2019).

I am not implying that there shouldn't be punishment or discipline as a parental response, but between two offended parties, the forgiveness should be applied sweetly and quickly.

 IF YOUR CHILDREN DON'T FORGIVE ONE ANOTHER, THEN THEY WILL SOMEDAY FIND IT IMPOSSIBLE TO FORGIVE THEIR SPOUSES OR OTHERS WHO HAVE WRONGED THEM.

As a parent, you must model forgiveness. When you have blown up in anger with one of the children, quickly repent and ask for forgiveness. Pray with the child who bore the wrath of your anger and then bless the child in some manner. When there is tension between you and your husband, take the time to talk about it and ask for forgiveness. If the children have heard the confrontation, make sure that they know mom and dad have forgiven each other.

> In the shadow of my hurt, forgiveness feels like a decision to reward my enemy. But in the shadow of the cross, forgiveness is merely a gift from one undeserving soul to another.
>
> —Andy Stanley

Forgiveness is when the innocent one lets the guilty one go free; forgiveness is never deserved but is always a gift of grace. If a child is struggling with the concept of forgiveness, share with this dear one a Bible story in which forgiveness was displayed, such as Joseph forgiving his brothers (see Genesis 45:4–8) or the parable of the prodigal son (see Luke 15:11–32). Or, read a biographical account of someone who chose to forgive in spite of cruelty.

Some children have an inner sense of justice that makes it hard for them to forgive. In this case, make sure that you take time to listen to your child's heart and help him or her process the obedience of forgiveness. Jesus taught us, *"Be merciful, just as your Father is merciful....Forgive, and you will be forgiven"* (Luke 6:36–37 NIV). We do not forgive because we *feel* like it but simply because we have been forgiven ourselves. It is, after all, what Jesus would do.

Forgiveness is a foundational issue of family life.

MAKE SURE THAT YOU TAKE TIME TO LISTEN TO YOUR CHILD'S HEART AND HELP HIM OR HER PROCESS THE OBEDIENCE OF FORGIVENESS.

Joy and Celebration

Oh, the fun that was experienced at our home over the years! When I think about the hysterical laughter, the holiday celebrations, the outrageous gifts that were given, and the raucous games that were played, my heart is filled with the satisfaction of a life well lived.

My goal as a mother was to have the happiest home on the entire street. Actually, I wanted to create the happiest home in the world, but I knew that it had to begin on our street. I realized that I would never be the richest mom or the skinniest mom, but I knew that I could be the most joyful mom!

Joy is the serious business of heaven. —C. S. Lewis

Children respond to joy and celebration; they come with an innate need to make merry and laugh with those they love the most and know the best. I endeavored to turn ordinary days into holidays and to discover opportunities to revel in every minute we were given together as a family.

If there was fun to be found, it was at our house. If there were games to be played, they were played around our kitchen table. If it was someone's birthday, everyone was invited. And if there was absolutely nothing to celebrate, I still served cookies and juice.

Joy, not grit, is the hallmark of holy obedience. We need to be light-hearted in what we do to avoid taking ourselves too seriously. It is a cheerful revolt against self and pride.

—Richard J. Foster

I wanted my children to know, from a very early age, that there was joy in serving Jesus. I wanted them to understand that we served a God of joy who was rejoicing over their lives daily.

The Lord your God in your midst, the Mighty One, will save; He will rejoice over you with gladness, He will quiet you with His love, He will rejoice over you with singing. —Zephaniah 3:17 NKJV

Life is hard, people can be cruel, and circumstances are often difficult, but joy will give your children the strength to get through the hard times in life. One of the greatest gifts you can give to your children is a mother who laughs often and who decorates their life with a selfless enthusiasm. If they remember nothing else about the house they called home, let them remember the joy!

Do not grieve, for the joy of the Lord is your strength.
—Nehemiah 8:10 NIV

Joy and celebration are foundational issues of family life.

Identity

It is within the safety of the family home that a child must know deeply who he or she has been created to be before the foundation of the world. Our children must know to whom they belong and they must also be acquainted with the Source of the love that is richly theirs to enjoy. We must teach our children the truth of who they are in the eyes and in the heart of the One who created each one.

The names that God calls you are the only ones you should be answering to. —Priscilla Shirer

When Craig and I had a new baby, we were given naming rights. My mom wasn't invited to name our children; the doctor who delivered the precious little one was not included in the conversation and neither were our neighbors! Craig and I had created this sweet mixture of his cowlick and my dimples and we were the ones who were given the honor of bestowing a fitting name upon this miniature piece of potential.

Our Creator has the naming rights of each one of us as well.

The Father has bestowed identity upon us and we must teach our children who God says they are before they begin to listen to the opinions of the world. Identity is most clearly established by the time a child is four or five years old so do not wait until the teenage years to begin to have this conversation with your children.

AS YOU ROCK YOUR BABY TO SLEEP, REMIND THIS LITTLE ONE THAT HE OR SHE IS COMPLETELY LOVED BY THE ONE WHO MADE THEM.

As you rock your baby to sleep, remind this little one that he or she is completely loved by the One who made them. Declare over your child that he is more than a conqueror in Christ Jesus. Affirm over your daughter that she is all glorious within and has been born for such a time as this. Repeat over your sons that they are chosen and free in Christ. Convey to your daughters that they are blessed and powerful.

Before I formed you in the womb I knew you, and before you were born I consecrated you; I have appointed you as a prophet to the nations. —Jeremiah 1:5

Identity begins with a declaration that's finally believed when it is repeated many times. Do not allow your children to forget what God thinks about them! When our children know and understand that they have been chosen specifically by the Father for a purpose and destiny at this time in history, they will no longer feel the need to have an identity crisis as a teenager. Instead, they will nestle into their God-given identity. Declaring this identity is a foundational issue in family life.

Encouragement

I believe that one of the greatest challenges a mother can face is making sure that her home is a place of lavish yet sincere encouragement. As you know by now, Craig and I raised five children; what I haven't mentioned before is that there was nearly fourteen years between the birth of the first child and the last.

All of my children were extremely verbal in the home and someone was always giving a strong opinion, making a request, or stating a fact…from their perspective. I am an introvert by nature so the constant communication tested my patience on many days.

When the barrage of words in my home reached a fever pitch and an accusatory tone arose, I would raise both hands in the air, which my children knew was a signal for, "Be quiet! Right now! Not one more word!" And into the silence, I would then calmly remind them, "In this house, we build up, we don't tear down. Were those building words or destructive words? Perhaps you would like to begin again."

Therefore, encourage one another and build one another up, just as you also are doing. —1 Thessalonians 5:11

There were days when I had to be firmer in my approach. In those moments, I said, "You may not say another word to your brother or your sister until it is a word of encouragement."

I was determined that our home would never lose its vision or purpose, which was to be a place of unconditional love and sweet encouragement. I also wanted to prepare my children for their own homes some day in which they would discover the joy that only a foundation of encouragement offers.

But encourage one another every day, as long as it is still called "today," so that none of you will be hardened by the deceitfulness of sin. —Hebrews 3:13

This particular verse was one of our oft-quoted Scriptures around the table, at bedtime, in family devotions, and during moments of play. When I asked my children, "What day is it?" they knew the only possible answer was "today," which meant that it was time to encourage someone in our midst.

We made it a delightful goal to encourage grandparents with homemade cards, neighbors with garden flowers, and the neighborhood kids with cookies and juice. Again, I knew that our home would never be the wealthiest home on the block but that we could be the most encouraging home.

I believe firmly that our words have unseen power; when we use our words as a source of encouragement, we are partnering with God in impacting a life for the better. My children were reminded that we were a family that was called to encourage others every day. I would tell them, "Be somebody who makes everybody feel like a somebody." And when I was tucking each one in at night, I would often ask, "Who did you encourage today?"

A word of encouragement during a failure is worth more than an hour of praise after success. —Willis Reed

Encouragement is a foundational issue in family life.

The Priority of Family

As your children grow, there will be many activities, people, and commitments that vie for their time and yours. However, as the builder of your home's foundation, you must make sure that family time is an immovable priority. As the mom, you are able to make this happen when you don't compromise the importance of family values or family gatherings.

Not abandoning our own meeting together, as is the habit of some people, but encouraging one another; and all the more as you see the day drawing near. —Hebrews 10:25

There is a reason why the early church called one another *brothers* and *sisters* and why we refer to our Creator as our Father. We belong to each other in the body of Christ and in God's family. Jesus declared, *"Whoever does God's will is my brother and sister and mother"* (Mark 3:35 NIV).

When your children are young, they will love the evenings that are reserved just for those who live at your home address, but as they grow, it will become more of a challenge.

Sometimes you will never know the value of a moment until it becomes a memory. —Theodor Geisel (Dr. Seuss)

We always scheduled family nights on Thursdays. The children knew that no matter what else was happening in their world, nothing trumped the gathering of the McLeod family. Homework was done early, the phone answering machine was turned on, and the evening belonged only to us. After a yummy meal, everyone helped to clean up so that Mama wasn't stuck in the kitchen. We would sing around the piano, play family games, or enjoy some other fun activity. Afterward, family night always ended with word gifts of encouragement and prayer.

Those evenings of family unity created a group of people who still love to gather, even today. My adult children now live thousands of miles apart, but they play family games on Zoom. They learned the beauty of the word *family* from an early age.

We are to grow up in all aspects into Him who is the head, that is, Christ, from whom the whole body, being fitted and held together by what every joint supplies, according to the proper working of each individual part, causes the growth of the body for the building up of itself in love.   —Ephesians 4:15–16

And this is the house we call home
though soon we'll be grown up and out on our own;
In the back of our minds we are never alone
When we think of the house we call home.[3]

---

3. Claire Cloninger and Nancy Gordon, "The House We Call Home," *Love Will Be Our Home* (Word Music & Church Resources, 1991).

4

The Nursery

For You created my innermost parts; You wove me in my mother's womb. I will give thanks to You, because I am awesomely and wonderfully made; wonderful are Your works, and my soul knows it very well. My frame was not hidden from You when I was made in secret, and skillfully formed in the depths of the earth; Your eyes have seen my formless substance; and in Your book were written all the days that were ordained for me, when as yet there was not one of them.

—Psalm 139:13–16

Shhh... Would you like to tiptoe into the nursery with me? Would you like to take a deep breath, gaze at the wonder of new life, listen to a lullaby or two, and then spend some time holding the baby? Would you?

The nursery is the room that is set aside for the dreaming of dreams and pausing to ponder the possibilities of all that might lie ahead. There are no to-do lists in the nursery, only the sweet realization of how temporary the purpose of a nursery actually is. You won't need a nursery forever but you will never forget the blessing of having one down a hallway in your heart. You will forever remember the smell of your baby's breath, the squeak of the rocking chair, the beatific gaze of those gentle eyes, and the songs that now are only distant melodies in your heart.

Don't be fooled by the peace that reigns in this nearly sacred room because behind the scenes, the hand of God is at work, shaping and forming a life for profound greatness. While the newborn baby is sleeping, God is commissioning His angels to be sent forth, setting up divine appointments, and designing a life of abundance and honor.

I hope that you have prepared a nursery in your heart, dear mother. I hope that you have a cherished place that is set aside not for doing but just for being. Don't neglect the nursery of your heart because in this quiet sanctuary, you just might spend the sweetest hours of your life.

DON'T NEGLECT THE NURSERY OF YOUR HEART BECAUSE IN THIS QUIET SANCTUARY, YOU JUST MIGHT SPEND THE SWEETEST HOURS OF YOUR LIFE.

The Dreaming of Dreams

When a woman steps across the threshold of motherhood, she doesn't stop dreaming dreams of life-changing destiny. She doesn't give up a call to greatness nor does she push away all the plans that she had imagined as a young girl. Oh, to be sure, this young mother's dreams might be altered just a bit and they even may be strengthened by waiting, but she will be a stronger, more creative mom if she spends time in the nursery of her heart, dreaming with the Father.

I have wanted to be an author ever since my teacher handed me a copy of Laura Ingalls Wilder's *Little House in the Big Woods* on my third day of second grade. I instantly fell in love with Laura, Mary, Carrie, and their good old bulldog Jack. Although I was only seven years old, I believed with my whole heart that I would write books someday. God placed that dream inside of me and it never waned or weakened.

When I became a mother, however, my focus was no longer on myself but on my precious children. I knew that as I developed their character and taught them about the call to greatness that each of them possessed, the Father would not forget my own call to live a life of impact. This was a lesson and a realization that I learned in the nursery of my heart.

As I pondered which dreams would be laid aside for a season and which dreams would become part of my life as a mom, the Lord tenderly began to speak to me about the seasons of a mother's life. *"To everything there is a season, a time for every purpose under heaven"* (Ecclesiastes 3:1 NKJV). We must identify exactly what season we are currently in so we can respond appropriately.

WE MUST IDENTIFY EXACTLY WHAT SEASON WE ARE CURRENTLY IN SO WE CAN RESPOND APPROPRIATELY.

If you are in the springtime of life, you should be planting flowers, not shoveling snow. If you are in an autumn season, you should be harvesting, not weeding.

So it is with motherhood; you must know what season of motherhood you are currently in and respond in the appropriate way. When you are up all night with a fussy baby, it is not the season to take a job that requires travel and ten- or twelve-hour days. When your children are teenagers and are finding identity in sports, piano recitals, and extracurricular activities, this will be the season to open your home to young moms for Bible study and encouragement.

Dreams don't come with an expiration date, dear mom. There will come a day and a time when the dreams of your youth will move to prominent priority. But know that for now, your dreams will be fulfilled as you nurture and care for the young lives that you have been given.

Many women now ask me what I did during those years of hands-on mothering to prepare for the life that I am living today. I am quick to reply that during those years of non-stop mothering, I read books, studied the Bible, and spent time in prayerful preparation for all that was to come. My dreams might have been set upon the shelf of my heart for a season but I didn't allow them to gather dust. I continued to write in my journals and listen for the voice of God.

Dream your dreams, dear mother! You don't stop living the day that you start nursing a baby. Your life will become richer and stronger when you give of yourself wholeheartedly to this beautiful yet short season. The day will come when your dreams are realized in a more exciting manner than you could have ever imagined. Believe me, I know!

Being a mother is not about what you gave up to have a child, but what you've gained from having one.   —Sunny Gupta

DREAM YOUR DREAMS, DEAR MOTHER! YOU DON'T STOP LIVING THE DAY THAT YOU START NURSING A BABY.

Intimacy

The nursery of a mother's heart is a place of intimacy that she has never before tapped into or even ever imagined.

You will know yourself in a fresh and timeless manner; you will enter into a relationship with another human being who, although only a few hours or days old, you feel as if you have known your entire life. It's also in the nursery of your heart that your dependency on your Creator is acknowledged as never before.

Intimacy isn't always automatic but it is developed over the hours and days spent in the company of a little person whose life has intersected with your own. If you do not automatically feel connected with your newborn baby, please don't panic. Give yourself time to get to know this brand new person so fresh from heaven. Remember that your baby is getting to know you as well! This is your baby's first journey outside your womb; everything and everyone is strange and unsettling. Hold your baby during these infant days, whisper words of love and kindness into the soul of the little life that's now your responsibility.

This time of sweet bonding is especially important if your blessing has been experienced through the miracle of adoption. A baby who was gifted to you from another woman, whose womb housed this child for nine months, may need extra time in your arms and against your skin. As you bond with this priceless treasure, know that you are establishing a relationship that no other person will ever have with this little one. As you bond with one another, his or her heart will belong to you in an intimate and unique manner. You chose this baby and the benefit of intimacy gained in the nursery of your heart is not just an endowment to the baby but to your soul as well.

 THE BENEFIT OF INTIMACY GAINED IN THE NURSERY OF YOUR HEART IS NOT JUST AN ENDOWMENT TO THE BABY BUT TO YOUR SOUL AS WELL.

Time spent in the nursery of your heart is not wasted time but it is time invested in the greatest treasure of your life.

I have certainly soothed and quieted my soul; like a weaned child resting against his mother, my soul within me is like a weaned child.
—Psalm 131:2

Bonding

I have a dear friend, Kathy, who has been a nurse in the NICU at Duke University Medical Center for many decades. Her job has included caring for the infants who are placed in this critical care unit due to conditions caused either by premature birth, serious illness, or the exposure to drugs or alcohol while in the mother's womb. My friend has increased her expertise as a specialized lactation consultant who helps new mothers with breastfeeding and bonding with their newborns.

One afternoon, as my friend and I were talking about our love for babies and the dear women who are nurturing the cherished infants, she happened to mention a condition known as failure to thrive (FTT). Babies are diagnosed with FTT when they don't gain weight and eventually lose their will to live. They are not hitting all of the significant milestones that babies are supposed to meet on their way to childhood.

The diagnosis of FTT is common in orphanages or in cultures where babies are not held, cared for, or stimulated emotionally, physically, and mentally. During our conversation, Kathy spoke as a mother, a well-educated nurse, an experienced caregiver, and a clinician to describe FTT.

Failure to thrive is simply the inability to sustain life, she explained. Many infants, for numerous reasons, are diagnosed with this condition. The most common reason for this diagnosis in full-term infants is the lack of food. Mothers water down the baby's formula or feed them less than six to eight times per day. Education is a major factor in helping parents realize that their child needs more food than is being offered.

THE CONDITION KNOWN AS FAILURE TO THRIVE IS COMMON IN ORPHANAGES OR IN CULTURES WHERE BABIES ARE NOT HELD, CARED FOR, OR STIMULATED.

While we continued our conversation, I could barely comprehend a mother not offering sufficient nutrition to a baby, but Kathy assured me that it happens more than we might suspect.

One of the truths that a mother needs to consider in the nursery of her heart is that all babies are different; what works for one may not work for another. When you, as a mom, are endeavoring to set a schedule for your tiny baby, consider the fact that not all babies possess a similar metabolic rate. Some babies need to eat every two hours while others are able to wait three or four hours. It has been my experience, in nursing five babies until they were twelve months old, that the cradling of the baby and the skin-to-skin contact are just as important as the nutrition that is offered.

If you are unable to nurse, or if you have been blessed with a sweet child due to the miracle of adoption, know that you can still offer your baby skin-to-skin contact as well as the snuggling that the baby so desperately desires and requires. Time spent with your baby as you gaze into his or her eyes, hold them close against your skin, and rub their tiny backs will be among the most beloved moments of your mothering experience.

Many mothers feel that they lack the time that it requires to spend time just holding and rocking their infant, but let me assure you that you don't have the time *not* to cuddle your baby. The security and the unconditional love that will be transferred during these moments will yield unmatched dividends in the years to come.

THE SECURITY AND THE UNCONDITIONAL LOVE THAT BABIES FEEL FROM CUDDLING WILL YIELD UNMATCHED DIVIDENDS IN THE YEARS TO COME.

As Kathy and I continued our heartfelt conversation, I asked her to explain the root cause of FTT. This was her guarded response:

> The biggest reason we see failure to thrive across the world is lack of personal skin-to-skin bonding. Infants in orphanages experience this condition at alarming rates because they are left in cribs for most of their infant days and are held rarely. These babies have learned not to cry to be held and are often viewed as "good" babies.

Do not be fooled, sweet mother. Just because your baby is not crying and is not demanding attention does not mean that he or she doesn't need it just as much as an infant who squalls his or her way into your arms. Babies come with one deep need when they are delivered to the arms and heart of a mother—they simply need to be loved. They need to hear your voice and feel your presence. They need to feel your arms around them and your heart beating close to them.

Kathy's true passion, birthed from years of observing mothering techniques and bonding issues with both healthy newborns and high-needs infants, embraces not only nutrition issues, physical limitations, and foreign challenges, but also the mistakes of our advanced culture. She says:

> Human beings are a carrying species, not a nesting species. American baby product companies are coming out with every

possible product to enable us *not* to hold our babies. Even some well-intentioned Christian books are written from the perspective that it will spoil your infant if you hold them rather than let them cry. Holding, cuddling and skin-to-skin contact are all mandatory for his/her physical well-being and mental health issues. Skin-to-skin contact, as seen every three hours with breastfeeding mothers—called "kangaroo care" in neonatal units—is as important as the food itself to the infant.

When infants are placed upon their mother's chest and their hearts are in proximity, the mother's core body temperature will go up to warm the infant. Her body will cause the infant's heart rate to regulate, his respirations to become normal, and regulate the infant's temperature. This intelligent design is perfect... not to mention the perfect nutrition offered by the breast, which happens to be next to the mother's heart.

Don't you just love that?! When you hold your baby close to your heart, you are able to bring health and well-being to your baby! We serve a perfect Creator whose delight it is to hold us and care for us as we grow in our faith. He is the example of how to tenderly guide a little one to safety and wholeness.

If you remember nothing else about this chapter, please remember this one thing: *you do not spoil a baby with love!* Children are spoiled when they are given an abundance of toys or treats, or when they are rarely disciplined as they grow. A newborn baby is not spoiled when the mother, father, grandparents, or older siblings spend time cooing over their little lives, singing to them, or even holding and rocking the precious baby throughout the day.

A NEWBORN BABY WILL NOT BE SPOILED WHEN YOU COO OVER THEM, SING TO THEM, OR HOLD AND ROCK THEM THROUGHOUT THE DAY.

As my babies grew, I realized that when they were about two months old, an inner switch was flipped in their little nervous systems and it was time to begin to work on a reasonable schedule for their age. My goal was always that by about three or four months in development, the baby would be eating about once every three hours and perhaps sleeping for about a five- or six-hour stretch at night. By the time the infant was six months old, I was hopeful that this little one was then comfortable enough with life to eat about once every four hours and sleep close to an eight-hour stretch at night before waking.

Enjoy these days, dear mother. Don't be hard on yourself or demanding of your baby. Cherish the days spent in the nursery of your heart.

Therefore, rid yourselves of all malice and all deceit and hypocrisy and envy and all slander, and like newborn babies, long for the pure milk of the word, so that by it you may grow in respect to salvation, if you have tasted the kindness of the Lord. —1 Peter 2:1–3

To Cry or Not to Cry

There is a popular parenting philosophy that espouses allowing your babies to cry themselves to sleep from the first day that you bring them home from the hospital. This ideology, birthed by Christians, even teaches that if you cannot bear to hear your infant cry, then go outside and wait for them to fall asleep.

I am aghast every time that I talk to a sweet mom who has bought into this system. It breaks my heart. Let me remind you that babies arrive on earth with one basic need: to be loved by the ones who are caring for them. Allowing an infant to cry himself or herself to sleep does not promote bonding or security within the child's soul.

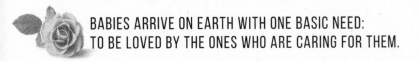

BABIES ARRIVE ON EARTH WITH ONE BASIC NEED:
TO BE LOVED BY THE ONES WHO ARE CARING FOR THEM.

I did not let my newborn babies cry themselves to sleep. I believe that babies need comfort, nurturing, and time in these formative months. I will admit that it wasn't easy to deal with a fussy baby in the middle of the night by holding, rocking, and patting. But neither is it easy to allow a baby to cry and keep the family up all night.

I believed then, and still do to this very day, that I would rather spend fifteen or twenty minutes rocking a sleepy baby than hearing his or her wails for an hour or more. The security that we give to a child by being available with comfort and compassion is part of the journey of motherhood.

I have had colicky babies and babies who refused to sleep. The best way to handle these unhappy infants was by holding them close to my skin, rocking them, and allowing them to hear the cadence of my voice.

Not Doing But Being

We live in a culture that exalts productivity, accomplishments, and achievements. We have believed the deception that busier is better and that in order to have a successful day, you must have checked every single thing off of your to-do list. It is in the nursery of your heart that you realize the value of *being* rather than *doing*.

Motherhood forced me to lay down my agenda and pick up the peaceful requirements that the Lord had for me as I gazed at the view in the nursery of my heart. As the consummate type-A personality, I struggled in the early days of motherhood. I loved my son deeply and was captivated by his little grunts, movements, and middle-of-the night snuggles. However, I was accustomed to functioning at a high level of daily accomplishment and expecting fairly immediate rewards for my diligence. The choice that I had made to now give the hours of my day to the chiefly unrecognized and even minimized vocation of motherhood challenged my sense of inner worth and responsibility.

 IN THE NURSERY OF MY HEART, I LAID DOWN MY AGENDA, MY TO-DO LIST, AND MY PERSONALITY BENT AND DISCOVERED AN ENTIRELY DIFFERENT WAY TO BECOME A SIGNIFICANT WOMAN.

I gave myself the time that I needed to settle into the new routines and unfamiliar expectations. Rather than reject my new reality as being less than meaningful, I patiently and sometimes hesitantly embraced all that was strange to me in this new lifestyle. My loving Creator patiently taught me that in His unshakable kingdom, *being* is always more valuable than *doing*. It was in the nursery of my heart that I laid down my agenda, my to-do list, and my personality bent and discovered an entirely different way of becoming a significant woman.

I learned, in the nursery of my heart, that cuddling a baby was more eternal than a conference phone call with the president of a prestigious company.

I learned that singing the hymns of childhood over my infant son was more prestigious than performing a piano concerto on the stage of Carnegie Hall.

I learned that rocking my baby to sleep was more satisfying than rocking the world with my achievements.

The hand that rocks the cradle rules the world.

—William Ross Wallace

The Little Things

The nursery is filled with little things, isn't it? It holds little bears and little clothes, tiny blankets and miniature books. It is in the nursery of your heart that you develop an appreciation for the little things in life and where you begin to understand that these are actually life's big things.

The nursery teaches that it is the little things in life that are capable of building a grand and historic life. So often, during other years of my life, I have made the glaring error of living for the big moments, for the red-letter days of graduations, weddings, and championship ball games. The nursery has taught me that those monstrous occasions, as fabulous as they might seem at the time, do not construct a vital and enchanting existence at all.

 THE NURSERY TEACHES THAT IT'S THE LITTLE THINGS IN LIFE THAT CONSTRUCT A VITAL AND ENCHANTING EXISTENCE.

A glass of iced tea on the back deck while the children are playing baseball, and the sweet giggle of a child just waking up from a nap—these give birth to a whimsical life. The smell of the roses as I walk to the front door, a good book and a cup of coffee on a rainy afternoon, and making cookies with the children to share with the neighbors—these build a life of grand and lasting proportions.

A glorious life is built one small but meaningful and carefully chosen building block at a time. A wonderful life is composed of long walks along country roads while the children gather wildflowers. It is pancakes on a Saturday morning and popcorn on Sunday evening.

In the nursery of my heart, I have been taught that the real stuff of life is as close and as dear as the morning song of the bird outside my bedroom window, the companionship of my daughter on my daily run, and the treasure of reading a devotional book that belonged to my grandfather. Those events may seem small and even inconsequential to you, but to me, they deliver joy.

There is no applause in a nursery, nor are there diplomas on the wall or trophies lined up across the changing table, but it remains the most splendid room in the entire home. The nursery is absent of the rush of adrenaline, but it is filled with the sweet sighs of contentment.

Make sure that your character is free from the love of money, being content with what you have; for He Himself has said, "I will never desert you, nor will I ever abandon you."   —Hebrews 13:5

We are reminded, by the wisdom of Paul, the great theologian, to learn the contentment that is found not in achieving but in belonging to Christ. Contentment is a learned behavior and is not a knee-jerk reaction to the monumental happenings in life. Contentment requires peaceful thoughts, listening to the stillness, and submitting oneself to the miracle of an ordinary day. All of this happens in the nursery of your heart.

For I have learned to be content in whatever circumstances I am.
                                                —Philippians 4:11

When I look back at the substance of living that created a healthy childhood for my children, I realize that it was ice pops on a hot summer day, laughing at a shared family joke, and praying every night before bed that brought security and happiness into our home.

To be sure, we cheered like fanatics at the championship ball games, I cried at five high school graduations, and we celebrated every birthday like royalty, but those moments did not define the life we had been given. What made life worthwhile was reading a book together in the evenings, catching fireflies in the backyard, and singing around the piano. Those simple yet valuable choices gave us a strong foundation of life at its finest and richest; this family philosophy was cultivated and treasured in the nursery of my heart.

WHAT MADE LIFE WORTHWHILE WAS READING A BOOK TOGETHER IN THE EVENINGS, CATCHING FIREFLIES IN THE BACKYARD, AND SINGING AROUND THE PIANO.

Perhaps living inside a regular day in which nothing of earth-moving significance happens is at the heart of all that is truly meaningful and extraordinary.

The glory of life is found quite simply in the ordinary moments. The treasure of a life well lived is acquired not in getting but in giving. The substance of all that is good, rich, and meaningful is found in a thousand inconsequential gifts that are easily overlooked if one is not careful.

I hope that you will treasure the time spent in the nursery of your heart and remember that it is the little things that contribute to a large life.

The Joy of Today

Do not boast about tomorrow, for you do not know what a day may bring. —Proverbs 27:1

As I linger in the nursery of my heart for just one more lesson, I am reminded that today is the very best day of my life. There is no richer or fuller gift than the undeserved endowment of the present.

What is without fiction or exaggeration is that I am able to choose how much splendor I will wring out of today. Will I slog through uncommon moments and look dull-eyed at all that I have been given? Or will I embrace the ordinary miracles that rear their lovely heads in every waking moment?

If my focus is fixed on the remote possibilities of tomorrow, I will never be captivated by the wonder of now!

Mom, if I could give you one more word of advice while we stroll through the nursery, it is this one: don't wish your child's life away by saying things like, "I can't wait till my baby sleeps through the night... or is potty-trained... or learns to talk... or goes to preschool."

Indulge in the amazement of parenting that belongs to you today. When you are up with a colicky baby, pray that this little heart will stay soft toward the Lord and that he or she will walk in their God-directed destiny in life! Don't waste time mourning over lost sleep but celebrate the quiet moments of prayer that are so vital to the person that this little life will someday become.

Treasure every season, every day, and every unscripted opportunity to pour love, time, and training into the child who will become the legacy that you leave behind.

---

*My mouth is filled with Your praise and with Your glory **all day long**.* —Psalm 71:8

The choices we make today determine the joy and love we will experience tomorrow. The investment of wholehearted engagement in the present will assuredly bring a wealth of resources tomorrow. However, the focus must be on living well *today*.

A new baby is like the beginning of all things—wonder, hope, a dream of possibilities. —Eda Leshan

5

The Classroom

Come to Me, all who are weary and burdened, and I will give you rest. Take My yoke upon you and learn from Me, for I am gentle and humble in heart, and you will find rest for your souls. For My yoke is comfortable, and My burden is light. —Matthew 11:28–30

I will always remember the feeling I had as a child that awakened in my heart the night before school began. The anticipation took on the grandiose expectation of Christmas Eve, my birthday, and the Fourth of July all rolled into one astonishing event. How I loved school and everything that it represented!

I loved freshly sharpened pencils, new notebooks, and the promise of walking into the library. I cherished lunch in the cafeteria with my friends, the bus ride in the early morning light, and learning a new locker combination. One of the reasons I had such a strong affection for school was because I discovered who I was born to be as an individual, as a learner, and as a young woman in the classroom.

In the classroom of your heart, you, too, just might identify the deep callings and purposes for which you have been born. In the classroom of your heart, you will ascertain your *why* and your *how*. If nothing else, motherhood is most certainly a challenging classroom in life. The lessons that are taught—and hopefully caught—in the classroom of your heart will equip you not only to be a better mother but also a wonderful wife, sister, daughter, and friend.

> I learned more about Christianity from my mother than from all the theologians in England.   —John Wesley

The Why

The day that you were born was a day of paramount importance. However, perhaps a day of greater impact and meaning is the day that you figure out *why* you were born. The discovery of your purpose in life, why God made you, and why history would be incomplete without the unique fingerprint of your heart is a day of unequaled significance in the life of any human being.

THE DAY THAT OUR FIRST SON WAS BORN, I HAD THE OVERWHELMING YET SWEET ASSURANCE THAT I HAD BEEN BORN TO BE A MOM.

The day that our first son was born, I had the overwhelming yet sweet assurance that I had been born to be a mom. I had found my purpose in life. Your purpose is not *just* a job nor is it merely a career appointment; it is your assignment from God. On that unforgettable day in my life, while my body was torn asunder, my mascara was everywhere except where it was supposed to be, and I was heaving for joy and relief, I heard the voice of my Creator whisper into my weary soul, "This is *why* I created you, Carol. This is *why* you were born."

I loved every single detail about being a first-time mother. I loved nibbling on his ten tiny toes and smelling his breath that was so fresh with the perfume of heaven. Craig and I raced to see who would be the first one to get up in the middle of the night when we heard his wee cry. We just couldn't get enough of this baby boy who was the tangible demonstration of our love for one another.

I loved to sing silly songs while nursing him and hear his first baby chortle. Is there anything as dear as the giggle of a baby who is drunk on love? Matthew took his first confident steps one Sunday night across the front of the church where my husband pastored. The entire congregation started cheering for this mix of Craig's athleticism and my cheerful outlook.

And then when Matthew Craig McLeod turned two years old, I discovered an even greater reality than *why* I was born. I was taught the *how* in the classroom of my heart.

> Life doesn't come with a manual. It comes with a mother.
> —*Good Housekeeping Magazine*

The How

Merely discovering one's destiny does not present enough information to ensure that you are able to live a life of divine purpose and power. To amplify the impact of your life, you need to know *how*. *How* you accomplish your destiny will add thematic essence and enthusiastic spirit to your life.

MERELY DISCOVERING ONE'S DESTINY DOES NOT PRESENT ENOUGH INFORMATION TO ENSURE THAT YOU ARE ABLE TO LIVE A LIFE OF DIVINE PURPOSE AND POWER. YOU NEED TO KNOW HOW.

I discovered my how in the winter of 1983. We had been snowed-in at our western New York home for over a week. We only had one car at the time, so I didn't even get out to go to the grocery store. I would give Craig a list in the morning and he did the shopping on his way home from work on those frigid winter afternoons. There were record-setting snowfalls that winter and I didn't dare try to go outside with a two-year-old and a brand new baby boy. Christopher Burton McLeod was born at the end of January that infamous year. He was up with colic every single night until he was nearly nine months old.

One particular cold, snowy day started out much the same as the other mornings of that historic winter. I made Matthew his simple breakfast of a scrambled egg and a side of applesauce. I was still wearing my robe and had not yet combed my hair or brushed my teeth. I was honestly just living one minute at a time.

The baby was crying and I knew I needed to change his diaper and nurse him. I also knew that I should take care of him quickly or the cries would get louder, more insistent, and more difficult to calm.

Matthew was singing, "It's a wonderful day in the neighborhood," while swinging his chubby little legs and enjoying his favorite breakfast. He reached for his tumbler of milk and accidentally hit the gallon of milk that I had inadvertently left on the table. That milk, which was supposed to last an entire week, went splashing over the table, onto Matthew's breakfast, and across my green linoleum floor that honestly had not been washed since before Christopher's birth. A week's worth of milk was now gone, my already messy house was now messier, and the baby was now screaming louder. I opened my mouth in anger and frustration while volatile tears ran down my tired cheeks.

I was simply out of control. Have any of you felt that way? I had not slept in months due to a miserable last trimester of a pregnancy that had lasted nearly ten months. I was hyperaware of my colicky four-week-old baby who was in constant pain; I had delivered that same nearly ten-pound baby just a month ago and the birth had ripped me from stem to stern. Finally, on top of the mountain of stress I was facing, we had no money for anything.

I SAT ON THE FLOOR, AN EMOTIONAL AND PHYSICAL MESS, AND WEPT AS IF MY HEART WERE BREAKING.

I sat on the floor, an emotional and physical mess, and wept as if my heart were breaking. Matthew, my precious two-year-old gift from God who I loved beyond measure, had been needlessly and profusely wounded by my anger, so he crawled into my arms and cried with me. Christopher was still in the other room screaming with pain and hunger. The wind was blowing against our windowpanes with an unending blizzard outside and I felt that God was crying with me as well.

We were all crying—Matthew, Christopher, the fierce weather, and me. I was an abysmal failure at the one thing that I felt called to do above all others. Oh, how I wanted to be a wonderful mother! But on this day, the wonder had slipped away with the gallon of milk. On this day, I could have been described as an angry mom, a frustrated mom, or an impatient mom. I didn't want to be any of those things.

In that moment, just like on the day of Matthew's birth, I heard the loving voice of the Father speak to my wintry, weary soul. As I recall, from the vantage point of over thirty-five years, He said something like this:

"Carol, you are a mom. It is who I have created you to be from the beginning of time. You can't change your call or destiny because you don't have that power. You can't change who you are. You are going to be a mom to these two little boys—and to others—for the rest of your life. From the day of Matthew's birth until you are called to heaven, your God-given identity is that you are a mom—a mother appointed by God at this moment in history! You are called to raise the next generation for Christ and His kingdom. But Carol, don't ignore the fact that you determine *how* you will do what I have called you to do. I can't choose your *how*—I can only determine the *what*. You, as a mother and as a child of God, must choose your own *how*."

That day, in the classroom of my heart, I was taught by my loving Father that the day of my birth was not my defining moment, nor was the day that I discovered my purpose the capstone of living. As I sat in a puddle of tears and milk, with a little boy in my arms, I realized that the one shining moment of my life was when I decided *how* I would fulfill my life's call.

It is in the classroom of your heart that you determine your *how*.

Adjective: any member of a class of words that modify nouns or pronouns, primarily by describing a particular quality of the word they are modifying, such as *wise* in *wise grandmother*.

You Choose Your Adjective

You are more defined by your *how* than you are by your *what*. I knew what I was: a mom. Motherhood was my calling, identity, and purpose; motherhood was my noun. However, I had been given the awesome responsibility of determining my *how*. My assignment from heaven's perspective was to regulate the how; I would select the adjective with which I would fulfill the calling of my life. God had designed me for motherhood, but I would decide what type of mom I would be.

IT IS IN THE CLASSROOM OF YOUR HEART THAT YOU CHOOSE WHAT KIND OF MOTHER YOU WILL BE.

I could choose to be an angry mom or a peaceful mom, a loud mom or a measured mom. I could decide to be a frustrated mom or a fulfilled mom, an impatient mom or a kind mom.

It is in the classroom of your heart, as a mother, that you choose your adjective. You are a mom and nothing will ever change that wonderful calling on your life. However, remind yourself often that you are the only person on the face of the planet who is able to determine what type of mother you will become or you are. Your past has not dictated that; we should never give our past that much power. Your income should not prescribe what kind of mother you are today; please do not give money that type of ruling power in your life. The state of your marriage should not control how you mother your children; you can choose to be a joyful, loving mother even when your marriage is in disarray.

Will you parent with peace, kindness, joy, and celebration? Or will you leave a legacy of anger, impatience, unreasonable demands, and strife in the wake of your years of mothering your children? You choose.

On that frosty February morning in 1983, I got up off the floor, gave my darling little Matthew some graham crackers and a banana, picked up my wailing newborn, and we all skipped into the living room with new purpose in my heart. I sat on the couch and nursed my starving baby while Matthew, who quickly forgave me, enjoyed playing with his blocks and cars.

I learned that I am the one who will choose the type of mother that I will be every morning of my life. I learned that I choose my adjective no matter what the circumstances may be. I choose.

No language can express the power and beauty and heroism of a mother's love. —Edwin Chapin

A Kind Mom

After the fiasco of that wintertide morning, I knew that one of the attributes I needed to develop in the classroom of my heart was kindness. Mom, as your mentor and your teacher, allow me to gently say to you that if you choose no other adjective, choose to be kind.

The teaching of kindness is on her tongue. —Proverbs 31:26

The word *teaching* from this well-known chapter of Scripture means "habit, custom, practice, or doctrine." Kindness should be so deeply engrained in your character that it always comes out of your mouth. There should never be a moment or a situation that instigates any response except genuine and sincere kindness.

I have learned through the years that my words are the primary way that I mother the children who have been given to me. Kindness should not only be apparent in the words that I choose to say but also in the manner in which I choose to say them.

For a cup brimful of sweet water cannot spill even one drop of bitter water, however suddenly jolted. —Amy Carmichael

It is often in our children's most difficult moments that they need to hear words of kindness and compassion from their mother. When your child is overreacting and is challenging your authority as a mother, be firm but be kind. Don't give in to childish emotions and elevated words just because your child is acting in that manner; someone must continue to be the adult. When your child is out of control and you are at the end of your emotional strength, please do not morph into Cruella de Vil, the Wicked Witch of the West, or a feminine version of Scrooge. Such behavior won't solve anything. When a mother reacts emotionally rather than responding with patience, she may become a deficit in her child's life rather than a benefit.

WHEN A MOTHER REACTS EMOTIONALLY RATHER THAN RESPONDING WITH PATIENCE, SHE MAY BECOME A DEFICIT IN HER CHILD'S LIFE RATHER THAN A BENEFIT.

Perhaps children need the kindness of their mother the most when they are struggling. Tell them:

- "I know this is hard but we are going to make it. I will love you always."

- "Listen, let's keep talking and trying. I am honored to be your mom and we can get through anything together."

- "There is nothing you can do to make me love you any less than I do today. There is nothing you can do to make me love you any more than I do today. My love for you is not based upon performance but upon relationship. I am your mom and I love you."

- "I believe that in your heart, you want to do the right thing. So let's talk about what the right thing is."

- "Let's pray together and then we will figure out a solution."

Every day during my years of hands-on mothering, before I even got out of bed, I would remind myself who I was: the kindest mom of my generation.

Do not let kindness and truth leave you; bind them around your neck, write them on the tablet of your heart. —Proverbs 3:3

In those early morning hours before the coffee pot was on and while the children were still nestled in their beds, I would declare from the warmth of my bed, "Kindness! You are not leaving me today! You are written on my heart! I will be the kindest mom in America today!"

The Kindest

The day before I began my freshman year in high school, my mom asked to have a conversation with me. We sat together on the red velvet love seat with royal blue pillows that adorned our piano room. My mom, who was known for a flair of beauty and elegance, spoke to me these very impressive words, "Now, Carol, as you begin your high school experience, I just want to tell you that you will not be the smartest girl in the freshman class."

My blue eyes were staring into her hazel eyes and I remember thinking, *But Mom, I might not be the smartest but I can work the hardest!*

She took my young hands in her own and then said, "Carol, I also want you to know that you will not be the prettiest girl in the freshman class."

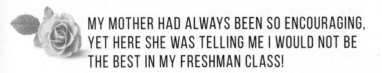

MY MOTHER HAD ALWAYS BEEN SO ENCOURAGING, YET HERE SHE WAS TELLING ME I WOULD NOT BE THE BEST IN MY FRESHMAN CLASS!

I couldn't imagine what had happened to my mother; she had always been so encouraging and the champion of everything that I undertook. *Had I done something wrong? Had I disappointed her in some way?*

My mom drew in a little closer and continued, "And, honey, you won't be the most athletic girl, the most musical girl, or the most popular girl in the freshman class."

My heart was in my throat and I couldn't imagine what was coming next. Although her tone was warm and compassionate, her words were causing me to question everything I hoped for or had dreamed about.

And then, my sparkling mom smiled. "But Carol, you can be the kindest girl in the freshman class and that is what I want your goal to be—to always be the kindest."

I took those words to heart at age fourteen and have never forgotten them in the five decades that have passed since that pivotal day in my life. My life's motto both then and now is, "To be the kindest."

What is desirable in a person is his kindness.   —Proverbs 19:22

One of the tenets of strong parenting is the truth that we are parenting for the long haul rather than just for the toddler years or to survive the preschool years. The foundation of kindness that you lay today in your relationship with your children will be able to withstand the pressure and challenges of the teenage years. If you desire a healthy, godly relationship with your teens in the future, then be kind to them today when they are little people. If you choose to attach the adjective *kind* to your job description, your teenagers will want to be with you and not be embarrassed about it. Even hormonal teenagers are unable to resist a truly kind person!

In the classroom of your heart, you learn to recite the following list of preferred mothering habits:

- Talk kindly

- Act in a kind manner

- Respond kindly

- Discipline kindly

- Train kindly

- Dole out kindness in large amounts

- Give kindness even when it is not deserved

There will be moments in mothering when you have to *put on* kindness because you will not feel like being kind nor will you want to be kind. There will be moments during the long days of mothering when all kindness has disappeared from your heart. In those days, you must *put it on.*

So, as those who have been chosen of God, holy and beloved, **put on** *a heart of compassion, kindness, humility, gentleness, and patience.*
                                                                        —Colossians 3:12

The Holy Spirit has given you permission to act kind even when you don't feel kind. As a mother, you must decide to put on kindness just like you choose what to wear in the morning. Kindness is a decision that weary, worn-out moms make every day in every season of mothering. When you don't feel kind, remind yourself that it is who you are. Kindness is not a feeling but it is a fruit and a choice. Kindness is not an emotion but it is a habit and it is surely also a practice.

> No act of kindness, no matter how small, is ever wasted.
>
> —Aesop

A Joyful Mom

The second adjective that I embraced as my very own in the classroom of my heart is the highly contagious word *joyful*. I can assure you that if you choose to be a joyful mom, your children will indeed rise up and bless you!

THE REPUTATION OF THE PROVERBS 31 WIFE AND MOTHER ECHOES THROUGH THE AGES. SHE IS MISS AMERICA, JOANNA GAINES, AND MOTHER TERESA ALL ROLLED INTO ONE.

The thirty-first chapter of the book of Proverbs has always been the text-book for women who want to honor God with their lives. There have been days when the Proverbs 31 woman intimidated me and other days when I didn't like her very much. We don't know her name, but her reputation echoes through the ages. She is Miss America, Joanna Gaines, and Mother Teresa all rolled into one overachieving woman. If this amazing woman were alive today, I can only imagine that she would win the Nobel Peace Prize, be named *Time* magazine's "Person of the Year," share her parenting expertise on *Good Morning America*, and invite everyone over for dinner—all on the same day!

After repenting for my bad attitude concerning this exemplary woman, I realized that I found in her something to admire.

She girds herself with strength.   —Proverbs 31:17 NKJV

Where did this woman obtain the strength that she needed to milk the goats, move the tent pegs, plant crops that would feed her family in the desert, sell fields for her husband's benefit, help those in need, make clothing, and raise an incredible family of young adults? Where does that kind of strength come from?

The joy of the LORD is your strength.   —Nehemiah 8:10 NIV

Although Proverbs 31 does not allude to the personality of this *"excellent wife,"* I can guarantee that she was a woman of perpetual joy. We learn she *"works with her hands in delight"* (verse 13) and *"smiles at the future"* (verse 25). Joy enabled her to be known as a woman of uncommon strength. Joy always precedes strength, not the other way around. If you are waiting to be joyful until you are strong, you have it all wrong, my sister in motherhood. Joy comes first and then the strength comes rushing in. If you are lacking strength today, perhaps what you need to do first is to cultivate the joy of your salvation.

Restore to me the joy of Your salvation, and sustain me with a willing spirit.   —Psalm 51:12

In Your presence is fullness of joy; in Your right hand there are pleasures forever.   —Psalm 16:11

Jesus is where the joy is so if you need more joy, what you actually need is more of Jesus. As a woman in the trenches of motherhood, you must spend time in His wonderful presence every day that you possibly can.

There is a marked difference between being a *strong woman* and a *woman of strength*. A strong woman is often intimidating and has an opinion on nearly everything known to mankind. A strong woman inevitably knows what to say, how to say it, and then always tackles inhuman tasks and completes them. A woman of strength, however, often demonstrates very differing character traits than those of a strong woman.

Trees that are known for their strength are also known for their fruit. For agriculturalists, the strength of a tree is determined by its root structure, its positioning, and the harvest of its fruit. If you want to be a woman of strength, you will position yourself by Jesus, the River of Life; if you long to be known as a woman of strength, then you allow your roots to go deeply into the richness of the Word of God. When you are known as a woman of strength, you will also be known as a woman who bears delicious fruit in all seasons of life.

 YOU BECOME A WOMAN OF STRENGTH BY POSITIONING YOURSELF BESIDE JESUS AND ROOTING YOURSELF IN THE WORD OF GOD.

But his delight is in the Law of the LORD, and on His Law he meditates day and night. He will be like a tree planted by streams of water, which yields its fruit in its season, and its leaf does not wither; and in whatever he does, he prospers. —Psalm 1:2–3

A Pink Bedroom

Our daughters will be like pillars carved to adorn a palace.
—Psalm 144:12 NIV

After three lively and energetic sons, the Lord blessed Craig and I with two delightful daughters who danced their way into our hearts with their own special brand of laughter, giggles, and sparkle.

I used to stare at our first daughter, Carolyn Joy—later christened Joy-Belle by her adoring brothers—in the middle of the night with tears streaming down my face. I just could not believe that I had the privilege of being her mother. And then, three years later, a second daughter, Joni Rebecca, was born to us and we named her after both of her grandmothers. I felt like a rich woman as I gazed into Joni Becca's blue eyes and smiled at the freckles that skipped across her dainty nose.

A daughter invites a mother's heart into a fairy tale of wonder and enchantment. Your days will be filled with tea parties, baby dolls, and ruffles. The door in your heart will be opened to the world of ballet shoes, princess paraphernalia, and maybe a soccer ball or two.

As a mother, you are responsible for raising a daughter of integrity and unrivaled virtue. The next generation of women will only be as honorable and remarkable as the women who raised them. Your calling and your identity become even more significant when you give birth to a daughter; you have been charged by the Creator to give back to Him a young woman with heaven seared in her soul. In our current culture of compromise and lackluster virtue, it is more important than ever to develop daughters who are bold, pure-hearted, and filled with godly identity.

 IN OUR CURRENT CULTURE, IT IS IMPORTANT TO DEVELOP DAUGHTERS WHO ARE BOLD, PURE-HEARTED, AND FILLED WITH GODLY IDENTITY.

Having raised both sons and daughters, I can assure you that your strategy will be the same at times and vastly different at other times. Raising sons requires perpetual energy; raising daughters requires perpetual creativity. In raising my sons to be great men, I often focused on the quest for both discipline and discipleship, while raising my daughters to be godly women demanded a winsome tenacity.

To Be Kind

My husband Craig was pastoring a growing church in North Carolina when our first daughter was born after our three frisky and spirited sons. The entire church body was thrilled that we would finally experience the enchantment of raising a little girl dressed in pink whose hair was bedecked in bows. As she grew into a toddler, the praise and compliments at church became effusive as she was passed from one grandmotherly figure to another, from one teenager to another, from one doting big brother to another. They would say:

- "Carol, she is just so pretty! I am so glad that you had a pretty little girl."

- "Isn't she just gorgeous? They don't make them like her, do they?"

I was concerned that my sweet little girl's disposition might turn prideful and pretentious from all of the flattery that she was hearing. I began to teach

Joy a lovely virtue that held lifelong meaning, "It's more important to be kind than to be pretty."

As I tucked Joy into bed every evening, I said to her, "Joy-Belle, is it more important to be pretty or to be kind?"

My dearly loved daughter looked into my eyes and said, "To be kind, mama, to be kind."

Teach your darling daughters the priceless virtue of kindness. Remind them often to be kind to their grandparents, their siblings, their friends, and people who might look differently than your family does. Instruct the precious young women who are growing up in your home to use only kind words, to have a kind expression on their faces, and to temper their voices with a kind inflection. Kindness is a splendid habit that will enable your daughter to live a truly significant life.

She opens her mouth in wisdom, and the teaching of kindness is on her tongue.   —Proverbs 31:26

Her Beautiful Body

One of the most important aspects of your assignment as the mother of a daughter is to begin to talk to her about her body and her appearance from a very young age. Let her know that she has been made in the image of her heavenly Father and her body is perfect just the way it is.

As she grows older, it is vital to talk to her about the necessity of protecting her body from the hands of others. I reminded my daughters often that they could talk to me about anything they wanted to talk about. There was no subject in our home that was off limits, even if it was a private subject. I wanted to be her first confidante in the matters of sex and her developing body.

 SET A STANDARD WITH YOUR DAUGHTER SO THAT SHE KNOWS HER BODY IS A GIFT FOR HER TO GIVE TO HER HUSBAND WHEN SHE IS MARRIED.

Set a standard with your daughter so that she knows her body is a gift for her to give to her husband when she is married. What a delight to be able to tell your sweet daughter that sex is beautiful within the glory of marriage and that waiting for that wonderful moment is worth it!

Her Needs

Although your daughter might believe she *needs* designer clothes, pedicures at age five, and $1,000 birthday parties, these are not what she actually needs in order to experience a memorable and happy childhood. What she needs is you, dear mom, and she needs much of you! She needs your time, your laughter, and your encouragement. She is aching for your words of confidence, your undivided attention, and eye-to-eye contact with you throughout the day. She yearns for uninterrupted moments just visiting with you and sharing the details of her day with you.

A CUP OF TEA AND A COOKIE WITH MAMA IS MORE MEANINGFUL THAN A MANICURE AT A HIGH-PRICED SPA OR A DAY SHOPPING WITH HER FRIENDS.

Mothers in our culture have sacrificed an intimate and dynamic relationship with their daughters on the altar of materialism. A cup of tea and a cookie with mama is more meaningful than a manicure at a high-priced spa or a day shopping with her friends could ever be. The opportunity for a little girl to share a secret with her mother or the delight that happens when you giggle with your daughter are priceless gems in the economy of love.

A daughter is a bundle of firsts that excite and delight, giggles that come from deep inside and are always contagious, everything wonderful and precious and your love for her knows no bounds.
                                                        —Barbara Cage

Walking hand in hand on a Sunday afternoon or awaking early to make pancakes together are representative of all that will shape the heart of your daughter before she enters the teenage years. If you want a loving, respectful relationship with your daughter when she is a teenager and a young adult, it begins by spending time together before she is old enough to tell you her needs.

A True Role Model

Our culture is an abysmal failure at offering wholesome, intelligent, and kind role models to our young women. The type of women whom your daughter admires when she is ten is the type of woman she will become. The culture idolizes women who are provocative, narcissistic, and materialistic. One need only to watch the Super Bowl halftime show or open a copy of *People* magazine to see such women. You can do better than the culture, mom!

As the mother in the home, you can present strong role models to your daughters—women like Elisabeth Elliot, Queen Esther, and Harriet Tubman. How wonderful to take the time to speak with your daughters about women such as the biblical heroine Deborah and the calling and commitment of Joan of Arc. I'll never forget reading the biographies of Corrie ten Boom, Mary McLeod Bethune, and Ruth Bell Graham with my daughters. By elevating true women of noble character and of godly virtue, you will minimize the type of influence that our culture has on your daughters.

Innocence

One of my goals as a mother was to keep my daughters as innocent as possible for as long as possible. This quest for purity in our home was reflected in the television shows and movies that we watched, the books that we read, and the music that we played.

We delighted in classic literature that promoted morality and substance of character; the entertainment that we enjoyed was filled with ethical actions and fortitude. The music that was heard daily through the rooms of our home filled our souls with cheerfulness, purpose, and joy.

THE CULTURE IS ON THE RAMPAGE, TRYING TO CAPTURE THE VERY SOULS OF OUR CHILDREN WITH SEXUAL PERVERSION, PROMISCUITY, AND IMMORALITY.

Innocence is a virtue worth fighting for but I must warn you that it will be an intense battle. You must never let down your defenses as you guard your daughter's thought life, her emotions, and any outside influences. The culture is on the rampage, trying to capture the very souls of our children with sexual perversion, promiscuity, and immorality. As the mother, you must fight with every resource, every ounce of creativity, and every prayer. Do not abort the call to raise daughters whose virtue is stellar and whose morality is immaculate.

> A babe in the house is a well-spring of pleasure, a messenger of peace and love, a resting place for innocence on earth, a link between angels and men. —Martin Fraquhar Tupper

Money Matters

One of the greatest gifts that you can give to your daughter's future husband and the children whom they will raise together is teaching her to budget her money well. It is an honor that we, as parents, are able to help our daughters understand the importance of tithing to the unshakable kingdom of God.

In our family home, we encouraged our children to tithe their monthly allowance as well as the extra money that they earned. We also taught them to save a portion of their income for larger purchases or experiences such as going to camp, a new bike, or a piece of furniture for their rooms. It is important to cultivate both patience and self-control in the lives of our children in the area of spending and saving.

OUR APPROACH TO FINANCES WITH OUR CHILDREN WAS SIMPLE: TITHING COMES FIRST, SAVING COMES SECOND, GIVING COMES THIRD, AND SPENDING IS LAST.

When an opportunity arose in which our family could bless someone in need, we always involved the children in the conversation:

- "Jesse's daddy just lost his job and we want to help the family out. Let's all pray about what we can do to bless our friends."

+ "I loved the missionary who spoke at church today, didn't you? Dad and I are praying about giving him some money so that he can bless his family. Would you pray with us?"

We never forced our children to give or made them feel guilty for not giving; we simply presented the opportunity and allowed the Holy Spirit to speak to our children's hearts.

Our approach to finances with our children was a simple one: tithing comes first, saving comes second, giving comes third, and spending is last.

Never spend your money before you have earned it.

—Thomas Jefferson

Modesty Matters

We live in a sex-driven society where even little girls dress provocatively and inappropriately. While I don't believe that our daughters need to dress like Pilgrims, I do believe that mothers must encourage our daughters to understand the importance of discreet clothing. There is a way to look smashing while dressing modestly. I believe it is even possible to be fashionable and conservative at the same time.

I learned in our family home that it was important to set these directives at the earliest possible age. If a young lady values her body, she won't feel the need to flaunt it. The fashion industry is intent on sexualizing girls—even in their toddler years!—but we, as noble women, should not be tempted nor should we acquiesce to the approach of Hollywood, New York, or Paris.

If the conversation about appropriate fashion begins early, it opens the door to shared opinions and the opportunity to pray and make decisions together, mother and daughter. One of the loveliest gifts you can give to your daughter is the gift of a guarded mind, a discerning eye, and a desire to dress in a manner that honors the Lord.

Modesty is the highest elegance.

—Coco Chanel

Emotional Stability

One Sunday afternoon when Joy was a teenager, she had a group of girls over, as she often did, so they could cook and bake together. On this particular day, while they were cooking up a delicious meal of chicken, brown rice with almonds, and our famous broccoli casserole, I was sitting at the computer, attempting to get ahead on my weekly work. As I was focused on the screen and the intense thoughts in my brain, Joy called out to me from across the room. "Come and talk to us, Mom."

When your teenage daughter invites you into her world of friends, you race to the occasion, which is what I did in that moment. As I approached the group of four young women, I said, "What do you want to talk about?"

"Talk to us about our emotions," was Joy's instant response. The reason that I could have this conversation with Joy and her friends was because Joy and I had been having the same conversation since she was just a little girl.

- "Joy, I know that you are sad but you can choose your happy heart."

- "Joy, you don't get to act like that. Take some time and pull yourself together."

- "Joy, you don't get to say everything you think, feel, or believe."

- "Joy, I know that your feelings were hurt but you can still be kind."

GIVE YOUR DAUGHTER THE TOOLS THAT SHE NEEDS TO PULL OUT THE EMOTIONAL WEEDS SO THAT HER LIFE IS A DISPLAY OF ALL THAT IS GODLY AND PLEASANT.

Our daughters long to know what to do with their emotions and how to handle the roller-coaster ride that emotions often predispose. I wanted to raise daughters who were not controlled by their emotions but knew how to control their emotions. Emotions are real but must not be allowed to rule your daughter's life. Give her the tools that she needs to pull out the emotional weeds so that her life is a display of all that is godly and pleasant. We must teach our daughters to make decisions based upon principle and not upon emotional preference.

Helping your daughter regulate her emotions will be a process that takes time. However, I can assure you that if she has a mother who has learned to have jurisdiction over out-of-control emotional responses to life, then she will model your example.

Watch over your heart with all diligence, for from it flow the springs of life. —Proverbs 4:23

Reach for the Stars!

As a little girl, when I was dreaming about becoming a teacher—and an author, a concert pianist, a nurse, a mother, and a stewardess—my enthusiastic mother would grin at me, take my face in her hands, and exclaim, "Carol, if you can't do it, there is no one who can do it!"

My mother's delight in my ability to dream outrageously big dreams laid a foundation in my life of imagination, diligence, and possibility. As a mother, remind yourself to listen to the dreams of your daughter's heart and never minimize her potential but always agree with her resourcefulness and inspiration.

My mom left little notes for me around the house, in my lunchbox, and tucked away in the books that I was reading. These encouraging notes said things like:

- Hitch your wagon to a star!

- Imagination is more important than knowledge.

- If you can dream it, you can do it!

HAVING A MOTHER WHO BELIEVES IN YOU CREATES A WOMAN WHO DREAMS WITHOUT INHIBITION AND BELIEVES WITHOUT RESTRAINT.

The simple fact that I had a mother who believed in me created a daughter who dreamed without inhibition and believed without restraint.

When I was in my phase of wanting to become a nurse when I grew up, my mother gently nudged me with these words, "You'd also make a wonderful doctor."

When being a teacher was my wholehearted goal, my mom smiled and mentioned without a pause, "I think you'd be a great school principal."

My mother stirred the dreams of childhood until they simmered into the possibilities of young adulthood. She knew when to pray, when to encourage, and when to give a push. You can do no less for the amazing woman who is growing up in your home.

> All that I am or hope to be, I owe to my angel Mother.
> —Abraham Lincoln

Grace Upon Grace

There is nothing more beautiful than a gracious woman. Grace begins its captivating process in the heart of a little girl through the instruction of her mother. Grace is not a shallow response to life but a deep, measured elegance that only the richest of women possess. It is a learned virtue that many times is manifested through disappointments or difficulties. A young woman who demonstrates grace is able to be thankful in the midst of turmoil, show generosity even in barren relationships, and continue to be a bedrock of stability when her world is uncertain.

Grace is a measured response that must be taught through leadership and by example. When your daughter doesn't get her own way, rather than allowing her to throw a tantrum or become sullen, teach her the fulfillment of an unselfish and thoughtful approach to life. When your daughter feels ignored by friends or rejected by others, allow her the joy of reaching out to someone who is also lonely.

A large facet of the deportment of grace is the ability to serve others rather than expecting to be served by others. Your daughter will be at her loveliest when she is giving to others, listening to others, and tending to others.

Grace is not a trait that magically appears overnight in a young girl's life; it is the result of years of training and observation. Your daughter's grace will only be cultivated by your grace because grace is contagious, passing from one generation to the next through observation and tender teaching.

YOUR DAUGHTER WILL BE AT HER LOVELIEST WHEN SHE IS GIVING TO OTHERS, LISTENING TO OTHERS, AND TENDING TO OTHERS.

Read Your Bible

If your daughter grows into a woman who values and honors the Word of God, then you will have accomplished eternal purpose as a mother. The Bible is able to do in your daughter's life what you are unable to accomplish. The Holy Spirit will speak to your daughter even when you are far away if she simply opens the sacred pages of the Scriptures. The greatest deposit you will ever make in your little girl's life is bequeathing her with the value that is found in the Bible.

When she is young, you can read it out loud to her and you can choose verses to memorize together or sing together. As she grows up, give her reading assignments on the Word of God and then discuss them together.

+ "What do you think Jesus meant when He said, *'Love your enemies'*?"

+ "Do you have any enemies? What is an enemy?"

+ "Why does the Bible say not to let the sun go down on your anger?"

+ "What does it mean to honor someone?"

The Bible is an active Book and it will do a rich and sustaining work in your daughter's heart that will cultivate the fruit of righteousness and joy. When you tuck her into bed at night, always ask, "Honey, did you read your Bible today?"

A mother's treasure is her daughter.   —Catherine Pulsifer

7

A Blue Bedroom

*All your sons will be taught by the LORD; and the well-being of your
sons will be great.* —Isaiah 54:13

I desperately desired a little girl during my first pregnancy. I thought that
I would be a perfect *girl mom*. I would love hosting tea parties, reading *Anne
of Green Gables* with a mini-me, and painting fingernails. My mother had
observed those intense and very verbal desires for the nearly nine months of
my pregnancy, and the night before I was to be induced, she called me one final
time and simply said, "Carol, little boys love their mamas."

How right she was! The next morning, when I gave birth to a perfect baby
boy, I had no disappointment but only delight!

The following day, as I sat in the rocking chair in my hospital room, holding the little man who heaven had selected especially for me, I started to weep
from the deepest part of me. Craig, who was sitting in a chair across the room,
looked up with concern etched on his handsome face.

"Carol, what's wrong?" he asked. "Is the baby breathing?"

I lifted my eyes away from the face of this already cherished son and with tears streaming down my cheeks, I gulped, "Someday, I am going to have to give him to another girl!"

Craig and I often laugh about that moment now but the reality is that from the first twenty-four hours of Matthew's life, I had the knowledge that I was not raising him for me or for my own selfish desires but I was raising him to love and serve someone else. I was raising a son to make a difference in the world, to lead his own home, and to make a lasting mark for the kingdom of God.

Little boys leave smudges on your heart.   —Art Moms

What Type of Son?

One of the very first questions that a mother must answer in the blue bedroom is, "What type of son do I want to raise?"

Perhaps you agree with me that we live in a world where men are struggling with their manhood and we need more men of intrepid honor and unremitting faithfulness. Our culture does not present wise or solid answers that enable a mother to chart a course of integrity and goodness for the sons whom she is raising. In the blue bedroom of our hearts, we mothers must determine that if nothing else, we will raise a good man, an honest man, a noble man. We must look to the Word of God and listen for the voice of our Creator as we partner with Him in the molding and shaping of the men who will lead the church, the nation, and the family in the next generation.

 IN THE BLUE BEDROOM OF OUR HEARTS, WE MOTHERS MUST DETERMINE THAT WE WILL RAISE A GOOD MAN, AN HONEST MAN, A NOBLE MAN.

Take some time to make a list of the attributes and virtues that you hope will describe your son in the coming years. What type of teenager would you like him to be known as? What characteristics do you desire for him to

embrace as a college student or young adult? What type of husband and father will he become, this little boy who loves frogs, robots, and chocolate milk?

The truth is that a boy becomes a man at the knee and at the heart of his mother. You have been given the authority and the creative intuition by his Creator to shape the masculine soul that seems so small and insignificant today. What will he become? He will become no more than his mother imagines that he will become.

> There is an enduring tenderness in the love of a mother to a son that transcends all other affections of the heart.
>
> —Washington Irving

A Humble Man

The chief and guiding virtue that a mother should instill in her son is the virtue of humility. Contrary to popular opinion in our culture, boys should not win every game they play nor should they be awarded a medal in every sport that they attempt. Your son should be taught from a very young age that a great person is a humble person.

Your preschooler can bring you a diaper while you are nursing the baby. He can say, "Please" and "Thank you" to his grandparents, and he can listen while Daddy is speaking.

 LOOK FOR WAYS TO ENCOURAGE OTHERS SO THAT YOUR SON DEVELOPS AN AWARENESS OF BEING A BLESSING EVERYWHERE HE GOES.

A mother should often remind her son to allow others to go first; she should teach him to encourage his friends and family members with his words. Demonstrate by your own example to look for ways to encourage others so that your son develops an awareness of being a blessing everywhere he goes. He'll learn to say things like:

- "Grandma, I like your dress."

- "You did a good job teaching our Sunday school class today, Miss Emily."
- "You kick that soccer ball great, Joey!"

The trophy of humility is the most important honor your son needs no matter what his age might be. We live in a world where athletes boast, entertainers crow about their accomplishments, and politicians preen. We need to create a generation of young men who will applaud vigorously for others and bow humbly to others whose skills and hard work have achieved a position of prominence.

Have your school-age son look up the meaning of humility and then commit it to memory. Encourage him to memorize Scriptures that reference the words *humble* or *humility*. Read biographies together that recount the life stories of men and women who lived truly great yet humble lives.

But the humble will inherit the land and will delight themselves in abundant prosperity. —Psalm 37:11

Manners Matter

Not long ago, my college roommate Debby and I had dinner at a family restaurant that is famous for its seafood and the view. A large family was entering the restaurant as we were leaving. The father opened the inner door for us and then turned around and said to his son, who was probably about six years old, "Chase, hold the door open for these fine ladies. It's what gentlemen do."

I turned to the father and said, "Thank you, sir. You are doing a great job with your son. I appreciate it."

The little boy looked at his dad with a grin that lit up the evening sky. As Debby and I walked away, I saw the responsible father give his son a high five, pick him up, and throw him in the air with a word of praise. This father knew what many parents ignore: manners matter.

Teach your sons to always let ladies and girls go first, open the door for others, wait for their turn in line, and honor the elderly. If you don't teach this future leader the manners that his career may require, who will do it? It is up to you, mom; it's not the responsibility of the school, the church, or his first boss.

TEACH YOUR SONS TO ALWAYS LET LADIES AND GIRLS GO FIRST, OPEN THE DOOR FOR OTHERS, WAIT FOR THEIR TURN IN LINE, AND HONOR THE ELDERLY.

We taught our sons that upon meeting someone new, they were to look that person directly in the eye, stick out their hand firmly, and say with cheerfulness and confidence, "Hi! My name is Jordan McLeod. It's so nice to meet you!"

Because your son is, after all, a boy, remind him often that gentlemen don't burp in public and that private matters should not be discussed in mixed company. As your son's mother, please do not tolerate racial slurs, mocking others, or sexual innuendos. Instruct your son that girls are always to be honored with his words, his actions, and in his thought life.

I believe that writing thank-you notes is not just for girls but is also a valuable skill for boys. When he is old enough, buy him some postage stamps and monogrammed note cards on which he can express his thanks for those who have blessed him in some way.

Although we raised some of our children in the North, where the requisite, "Yes, ma'am" and "Yes, sir" are not expected, they were still taught to use these polite forms of address. They were reminded daily that the courteous response to a man older than themselves was, "Yes, sir" or "No, sir."

As you teach your son the value of manners and honoring others, he will grow into a young man who himself is honored by others. Isn't that what every mother wants?

Prove yourself brave, truthful and unselfish, and someday, you will be a real boy.   —The Blue Fairy from Disney's *Pinocchio*

But, Mom! I Just Want You!

The countercultural truth is this, dear mom: your son needs you and your daily presence in his young life more than you could ever imagine or anticipate. He doesn't need another toy, more screen time, or designer athletic shoes. He doesn't need trips to Disney World or a brand new car when he turns sixteen years old. He needs *you*.

THE TRUTH IS, YOUR SON NEEDS YOU AND YOUR DAILY PRESENCE IN HIS YOUNG LIFE MORE THAN YOU COULD EVER IMAGINE.

One of my friends told me that every time her daughter, who is a young mom, leaves the house—whether it is for work, grocery shopping, going to a meeting, or just taking a walk—her little boy stands at the top of the apartment stairs and reminds her, "But, Mom! I just want you!"

The day will come quickly when your little boy grows into a big boy and he will no longer want you. He may even act like he doesn't need you. I know that in the season of 3 a.m. feedings, potty training, and grilled cheese sandwiches, that day seems eons away but it is not. That day will come tomorrow.

Little boys need their mom to talk to them about bugs and the solar system; they need their mom to build Lego creations with them and throw the ball in the front yard with them.

School-age boys need their mom to read to them and do science projects with them. They need their mom to fix nutritious meals and teach them to make their beds.

High school boys need their mom to talk about dating and their future plans.

All boys need the attention, the coaching, and the heart of their mom on a consistent and daily basis. They need their mom to pray with them every single day.

> Little boys should never be sent to bed. They always wake up a
> day older.
> —Peter Pan

Money Matters

I know that life can become so busy in the years of ball games, dentist appointments, homework assignments, and birthday parties, but please remember to teach your son to manage his money well. Money management and budgeting are among the greatest gifts you can give to your son's future family.

A little boy who receives an allowance or is given money for birthday gifts is old enough to learn the principles of saving and tithing. Don't give your son everything that he wants but teach him to save his money for significant purchases. When he is old enough, talk to him about creating a reasonable budget that will help him in years to come.

Our boys started working part-time jobs as soon as they were able to do so. They mowed lawns, helped their grandparents, and did pet sitting from an early age. As they got older, they cleaned the church, worked at a Christian bookstore, and did yard work at their school.

Young men need to know the value of working hard and saving their money for future expenses. They also need to be taught, in word and in example, the delight of tithing and giving to the kingdom of God.

Dream a Big Dream

Little boys carry in their massive hearts all of the potential of tomorrow. They are charged, by the God who created them, to dream dreams that are more massive than their imaginations, more colossal than the dreams of their fathers, and more immense than their culture tells them they should conceive.

 ALWAYS ASK YOUR SON WHAT HE WANTS TO BE WHEN HE GROWS UP AND SHOW ENTHUSIASM AND CONFIDENCE IN HIS PLANS.

From the time he is able to string words together, ask your son what he wants to be when he grows up. Bequeath to your son the power of your enthusiasm and your confidence in his plans.

"Son, what do you want to be when you grow up?" is a question that must be posed often to the little man who temporarily lives within the walls of your home.

Now, as a grandmother, every time that I take one of my grandsons out to lunch or to the park, I ask him that question. I deeply long to be part of his thinking and dreaming process even though we are two generations apart.

If your son wants to be a missionary, you should consider studying other cultures and languages with him so that he is prepared for the calling that lies ahead. Invite missionaries into your home, read books, and watch movies about men and women who served the Lord on continents far away from home. When possible, have a missionary over for dinner to tell the tales that your son's heart is longing to hear. Involve your son in trying out recipes from other countries. Develop his taste buds to prepare him for a life where food is decidedly un-American.

If your miniature man says he wants to be a firefighter when he grows up, take him to visit the local fire station. Be sure that you take those local heroes a treat from your kitchen or a local bakery and allow your son to present it to them. Depending upon his age, have him prepare some questions that he can ask the firefighters. When you arrive back home, have him write an essay or draw a picture about what he learned.

If your son is drawn toward the business world, encourage entrepreneurship from a very young age. Lemonade stands, family yard sales, a pet-walking service, and a lawn-mowing business should all be part of his growing up years.

Whatever he is talking about becoming, read books on the topic with him and invite people into your home who have built a career in that particular calling.

The most important part of your son's journey into dreaming his dreams with God is your support and your constant prayers.

When I was very young, most of my childhood heroes wore capes, flew through the air, or picked up buildings with one arm. They were spectacular and got a lot of attention. But as I grew, my heroes changed, so that now I can honestly say that anyone who does anything to help a child is a hero to me.

—Fred Rogers

Minor Does Not Equal Major

The week before Craig and I were married, we spent an afternoon with an elderly couple who were well-respected prayer warriors in the very small town in which I grew up. Among the two hundred inhabitants of my community, Mr. and Mrs. Houston were legendary for their beautiful gardens, their sunny personalities, and their commitment to prayer. Though they never had any children of their own, their home had a steady stream of children in and out the back door for an afternoon of crafts, checkers, Bible study, or cookies. It seemed only natural that before I married the man of my dreams, we would check in with these beloved sages who had modeled a life of service and sacred living.

When we asked them what word of advice they would give to us as we started on this grand adventure known as marriage, Mr. Houston said without hesitation, "Keep the minor things minor."

 "KEEP THE MINOR THINGS MINOR." THESE FIVE SIMPLE WORDS HAVE FORTIFIED OUR MARRIAGE AND OUR CHILDREN'S LIVES.

These five simple words have foundationally fortified not only our marriage but also our children's lives.

When one of our sons failed to hit the ball in a front yard baseball game, rather than allowing him to throw the bat down, kick the dirt, or have a sour expression on his handsome little face, he was reminded, "Keep the minor things minor."

When a younger sibling was allowed to choose the family movie, rather than be resentful or offended, the older brother was encouraged to, "Keep the minor things minor."

When there was only one ice pop left or the older boys were given a smaller piece of cake than the younger children, we told them, "Keep the minor things minor."

I will hasten to add that we looked for opportunities to bless our sons for being selfless big brothers and embracing godly heart attitudes so that their life was not one continual desert lacking any personal delight. However, we knew that we were called to raise sons who must not be allowed to overreact to minor disappointments and small challenges.

The five-word philosophy given to Craig and me by that precious older couple has served our marriage well, has helped us to raise five healthy children, and is now often heard in our children's homes.

Born to Be a Hero

Boys come pre-wired by their Creator with a longing to protect the people they love, slay dragons, and conquer kingdoms. If they are not given a vision for the nobility of this call, they will default to fighting the wrong battles and using this innate desire for harm rather than for good. A mother is able to offer her son the substance of a true hero. She has the capability of channeling his adventurous spirit into searching for good in every situation of life. A mother can teach her little boy to fight evil and be a heroic demonstration of all that is righteous and kind.

A mother must choose well the books that her son reads and the movies that he is allowed to watch. She must provide him with exciting examples of the virtues of honesty, wisdom, and servanthood. She is able to accomplish this fete by reading biographies of great men and women and heroic tales written by such men as J. R. R. Tolkien, C. S. Lewis, G. A. Henty, and G. K. Chesterton. At the dinner table, you can feed not only their young bodies but also their young souls by the conversations concerning what makes a hero, what it means to champion a cause, and what character traits make a man virtuous.

If you can convince your son that he has been born to be a hero in the truest sense, you will have raised a young man of honor and courage.

My brothers, I see in your eyes the same fear that would take the heart of me. A day may come when the courage of men fails, when we forsake our friends and break all bonds of fellowship, but it is not this day. An hour of wolves and shattered shields when the Age of Men comes crashing down, but it is not this day! This day we fight! By all that you hold dear on this good earth, I bid you stand.

—Aragorn in Tolkien's *The Return of the King*

Matters of the Heart

Shortly before your son reaches his tenth birthday is the time to talk to him about dating and his feelings toward young ladies. Although you are not ready for it yet, he is on the verge of being ready for it and might be more interested than you can imagine.

YOU MUST TALK TO YOUR SON ABOUT GIRLS WHILE HE IS STILL YOUNG ENOUGH TO THINK HIS MOM IS JUST ABOUT PERFECT.

You must begin this conversation before it is laced with embarrassment and adolescent emotion. When your son is ten years old, he is at the height of thinking that his mom is just about perfect so anything that you say at this age will be absorbed completely and believed fully.

Even if he has shown no interest in girls yet, he will soon! For single moms, it is of vital importance to remind him often that he can talk to you about anything—from body odor to facial hair to the feelings that he has for girls. My husband was the parent assigned to speak with our sons about sex, but Craig and I both let them know that they could ask either of us anything.

Teach your son to honor young ladies with his words, his thought life, and with his physical actions. You must talk to him about the strong feelings that he is apt to have for girls and how those feelings will impact his thought life and his choices. As he grows into a teen and the conversation continues, as his mother and as his first love, be involved in helping him to set boundaries in his affections and in his physical relationship with a young lady.

A Faithful Man

You are raising your son in a day and age in which faithfulness is not esteemed and when everyone from politicians to the media to business leaders scoff at the truth. However, as the mothers who are raising the next generation of boys to grow into men of uncommon value and unmatched virtue, we must teach our sons to be faithful champions and warriors for truth.

Teach your son the high privilege of cultivating the seed of faithfulness in his life and the power he holds when he keeps his given word. If he says that he will do something, then he must follow through. If he borrows money, he must pay it back. If he makes a commitment to a friend, a team, or at church, tell him that his word is his bond.

As God has given us sons to raise, it is up to us as their mothers to teach that truth is more valuable than gold, an Ivy League education, or winning a championship ball game.

> Whoever is careless with the truth in small matters cannot be trusted with important matters.   —Albert Einstein

Have You Read Your Bible Today?

Perhaps the most important discipline that a mother can encourage in the life of her son is making a daily commitment to the Word of God. When he is just a baby, it is vital that you quote the Word over him as you are nursing him, rocking him, and putting him to bed.

> *Do not be afraid, little flock, because your Father has chosen to give you the kingdom.*   —Luke 12:32

> *Jesus said, "Let the little children come to me, and do not hinder them, for the kingdom of heaven belongs to such as these."*   —Matthew 19:14 NIV

> *For God so loved the world, that He gave His only Son, so that everyone who believes in Him will not perish, but have eternal life.*   —John 3:16

As your son grows into understanding the words that you are speaking over him, take time every day to remind him what the Bible says about boys and how they should act.

Children, obey your parents in the Lord, for this is right.
—Ephesians 6:1

Be kind to one another, compassionate, forgiving each other, just as God in Christ also has forgiven you.   —Ephesians 4:32

For God has not given us a spirit of fear, but of power and of love and of a sound mind.   —2 Timothy 1:7 NKJV

It is inevitable that your son will encounter challenges in life; he will need more than his mom's advice to help him navigate the rough waters of circumstantial storms. He will need the Word of God deeply hidden within his heart to enable him to honor God no matter what journey life takes him on.

How can a young man keep his way pure? By keeping it according to Your word.   —Psalm 119:9

Jesus said to [the young man], "If you want to be complete, go and sell your possessions and give to the poor, and you will have treasure in heaven; and come, follow Me."   —Matthew 19:21

For the kingdom of God is not eating and drinking, but righteousness and peace and joy in the Holy Spirit.   —Romans 14:17

But it is not this way among you; rather, whoever wants to become prominent among you shall be your servant.   —Mark 10:43

Buy your sons age-appropriate Bibles as well as devotionals that focus on the hearts of boys and the issues that they face. I tried never to use the Bible for punishment, only for encouragement and discipleship. Please don't threaten your sons with the Bible but provide it as a compass for their souls.

As your precious little boy grows in knowledge and, like Jesus, *"in wisdom and stature, and in favor with God and man"* (Luke 2:52 NIV), give him his own copy of the Bible with his name engraved on the front. As you plan the moment that you will give him this treasured gift, have other family members or friends write a note telling him what the Bible has meant in their lives. Underline a few verses in his Bible and initial them so that he knows what his mom and dad's favorite verses were.

By the age of about nine or ten years old, every time that I tucked my budding lad into his bed at night, my final words of the day were always the same, "I love you and I believe in you. Did you read your Bible today?"

> The Bible is the book of my life. It's the book I live with, the book I live by, the book I want to die by.   —N. T. Wright

8

The Corner

---

*For the moment, all discipline seems not to be pleasant, but painful;
yet to those who have been trained by it, afterward it yields the peaceful fruit of righteousness.* —Hebrews 12:11

Whoever in the world thought that sending a lively little boy or an active, precocious girl to the corner would somehow improve their behavioral issues? What an utterly ludicrous idea to presume that requiring a child to spend any amount of time staring at the corner and the dust particles found therein will correct their lack of discipline or erase their inability to obey!

Discipline is one of the most difficult aspects of parenting at nearly every age of child development. What works for one child may simply not work for another because discipline is not one size fits all. Although the Bible certainly presents principles when it comes to teaching and training our children, as the mother of a unique child, you must realize that just as God gathers each one of us to His heart using different methods so it is with mothering and discipline.

Some of my children were corrected with just one look or by hearing their name said in a quiet yet firm way. However, this was not true with every child that I had the pleasure of parenting.

Discipline is never just about the moment that the infraction occurs. A mother must take into consideration the training that has been given to prepare the child for the crossroads of behavior and obedience as well as acknowledge the physical distractions that might play a role in their defiance, such as tiredness, hunger, or too much sugar.

A MOTHER SHOULD ALWAYS DEFAULT TO NURTURE, TRAINING, AND DISCIPLINE AS SHE ATTEMPTS TO RAISE HER CHILDREN SO THAT THEY OBEY TO THE BEST OF THEIR ABILITY.

There are three powerful words that a mother should always default to as she attempts to raise her children in an environment that enables a child to obey to the best of his or her ability. These three words are *nurture, training,* and *discipline*. Each word is unique and requires a purposeful response to a child's behavior, but these three strategies when combined will allow you, as a mother, to oversee your child's character development and conduct with love, strength, and authority.

Nurture

How lovely that the manner in which your relationship begins with your children is that you are the one who nurtures them, nestles with them, and comforts them. You are the one chosen by God the Father to tenderly care for the little one who is incapable of doing anything by himself or herself. You are the one who has been appointed to gently guide your baby and gather the vulnerable child in your arms. After all, this is how our loving and merciful Father treats His children.

---

*He **tends** his flock like a shepherd: he gathers the lambs in his arms and carries them close to his heart; he gently leads those that have young.* —Isaiah 40:11 NIV

I chose to memorize this verse when I was a young mother who had been up all night, had spit-up on her shoulders, and who barely knew her own name most days. When I was discouraged over the lack of order in my home or by the constant demands of motherhood, I would remind myself that my job was to treat my children with the same gentleness and love that my Father had shown me. When I was at the end of my emotional rope due to two-year-old tantrums, potty training, and lack of time alone, I defaulted to behavior that was not of my own making but came from the example of the Good Shepherd.

The word *tend* in this familiar Scripture can be defined as "to be companions, to be a special friend, to care for, to guard, to look after." What a beautiful way to describe the job description of a mother!

YOU DON'T SPOIL A BABY OR A CHILD WITH LOVING AND TENDER CARE; YOU SPOIL THEM WITH THINGS.

If you forget everything that I have written in this book and only are impacted by one single statement, please let it be this one: *You don't spoil a baby or a child with loving and tender care; you spoil them with things.*

This philosophy of nurturing, holding, and pouring tenderness into the life of your baby is so dear to my heart that I will remind you of it over and over again.

Babies come with only one need in life: they need to be loved and nurtured. God looked at all of the mothers over the face of the planet and He placed your little ones in your arms. Whether you are the mother of a colicky baby, a special needs baby, a strong-willed two-year-old, or a defiant teenager, God will give you the strength that you need to love and nurture.

If the aim of parents is to teach their children to love God they must show their love for Him by loving each other and loving the children. The process of shaping the child, shapes also the mother herself.   —Elisabeth Elliot

God's plan is that His very character would be translated from His heart to your heart during your motherhood journey. He wants you to treat your children the same way that He has treated you. His grace is enough for every long night and for every tear. His strength is available to a weary mother twenty-four hours a day, seven days a week. His compassion never wanes and He never runs out of lovingkindness.

But He gives a greater grace.   —James 4:6

The desire that a newborn has to be loved, nurtured, and kept safe is stronger than their instinct to suck or to nurse. You are the one who has been charged with the oversight of your little flock of children and you must model the character of God as you lead them.

---

*He tends his flock like a shepherd: he **gathers** the lambs in his arms and carries them close to his heart; he gently leads those that have young.*   —Isaiah 40:11 NIV

The word *gather* in this passage of Scripture means "to touch, to bring close to, to take hold of." As mothers, we are expected to treat our dear children in the same manner that the Lord has taken care of us. We need to hold our babies, bring them close to us, and touch them often and gently.

In the most advanced intensive care units in the world, when a premature baby with an erratic heartbeat and irregular breathing is struggling to survive, the expert staff places the infant on the mother's or father's chest for skin-to-skin contact. Often, precisely as this happens, the baby will begin to breathe regularly and his or her heartbeat will match the parent's.

 WHEN YOUR LITTLE ONES ARE MISBEHAVING OR FRACTIOUS IN BEHAVIOR, THEY MIGHT SIMPLY NEED YOU TO SPEAK KINDLY AND GENTLY WHILE YOU HOLD THEM.

Do you gather your children to you or do you keep them at arm's length? When they are misbehaving or fractious in behavior, what your little one might need is for you to gather him or her to yourself as you speak kindly and gently and lovingly stroke their back.

There is a need in every child, placed there by the Father, to be held, to be comforted, to be gathered, and to be touched. God touches us when we are disobedient and filled with pain; God holds us when we feel out of sorts or are angry. If this is what God does for His difficult children, it is what we should do for our little ones.

Or do you think lightly of the riches of His kindness and restraint and patience, not knowing that the kindness of God leads you to repentance?   —Romans 2:4

The prophet Isaiah reminded the people of God thousands of years ago that we have a Father who knows the value of carrying them close to His heart. The word *carry* is defined from its Hebrew roots as "to help, to aid, to touch, to support and to desire." How wonderful to know that your Father desires you! He longs to touch you and support you in your weakness, to aid you in your challenges, and to help you live in a place of hope and peace. As the mother of your children, that should be your desire as well: to *carry* your little one through the rough days and challenging moments in life.

Isaiah 40:11 also presents the picture that the Lord *"gently leads"* His children, which is the notion of tender daily care and protection from dangers and fears in life. The word that Isaiah was prompted by the Holy Spirit to use in this soothing verse is the same word that King David used in Psalm 23:2: *"He leads me beside the still waters"* (NKJV).

Dear mother, the same tenderness with which the Father holds us and cares for us in our pain, our discomfort, and our fears is how we are to treat our own little flock.

If I cannot give my children a perfect mother I can at least give them more of the one they've got—and make that one more loving. I will be available. I will take time to listen, time to play, time to be home when they arrive from school, time to counsel and encourage.   —Ruth Bell Graham

Will your nights be long and frustrating? Absolutely they will! Will the days seem to never end? Without a doubt, there will be days when your nerves are jagged and your resolve is tested. Will your heart and your mind grow weary? Assuredly you will long for a day off or just one night of uninterrupted sleep. However, I can tell you from my perspective as I look in the rearview mirror at my early days of mothering that the one thing I do not regret is the sweet nurturing of my children. I am filled with deep peace and satisfaction as I recall the times that I sang to them rather than shouted at them. I can rest in spite of my imperfections when I remember carrying my babies rather than allowing them to cry it out. I refuse to believe that encouraging toddlers in a soft voice was the wrong strategy in parenting.

I REFUSE TO BELIEVE THAT ENCOURAGING TODDLERS IN A SOFT VOICE WAS THE WRONG STRATEGY IN PARENTING.

The stirring truth is that in order to nurture your little flock in the same manner that the Father has nurtured you, you must know His character. You must take the time to get to know who He really is so that you can become like Him and embrace His strategies as your very own.

If you view God as an angry, harsh taskmaster who is ready to clobber you over the head whenever you get out of line, you will never discover the joy that nurturing your little ones will bring to your heart.

The choice to nurture your children establishes a solid foundation for the other two components of discipline. *Nurture* does not mean spoil. It means spending time with your children, listening to their little hearts, giving them hugs and kisses, and enjoying being with them. Do you recall the information that I shared with you in the nursery of your heart? We are a carrying species, not a nesting species, but our culture is presenting every contraption possible to make it easy to not hold our babies. It is important for a mother to remind herself often that holding a child, cuddling an unhappy baby, and even skin-to-skin contact are all mandatory for the physical and mental well-being of the little one.

Aren't you glad to know that when you run to the Father, He never turns you away? The Father's arms are always open wide for a child who is fearful or in pain. If you develop the gentle yet strong bond that nurturing your children will foster, it has been my experience that training and even discipline might become an easy part of parenting for you. Children who know that they are safe and loved respond much more effectively to their mother's training and, when necessary, her discipline.

NURTURE MEANS SPENDING TIME WITH YOUR CHILDREN, LISTENING TO THEIR LITTLE HEARTS, GIVING THEM HUGS AND KISSES, AND ENJOYING BEING WITH THEM.

When my children were teenagers, I wanted them to believe in the love and goodness of God that they saw modeled in their mother's heart during their formative years.

Love and obedience go hand in hand. Jesus put it this way: *"If you love Me, you will keep My commandments"* (John 14:15).

John, the beloved apostle, repeated this same approach to obedience.

And this is love, that we walk according to His commandments. This is the commandment, just as you have heard from the beginning, that you are to walk in it. —2 John 1:6

Obedience always springs forth from a love relationship. If you want your children to honor you and obey you as they grow into young adults, you will deeply love and nurture them when they are little. As a mother, I knew I was pursuing their hearts, not robotic behavior. I refused to allow our home to be focused on legalism, rules, and regulations. There were expectations, of course, but I endeavored to build a home were love was abundant, affection was actively demonstrated, and grace was lavished.

The best way to get children to do what you want is to spend time with them before disciplinary problems occur—having fun together and enjoying mutual laughter and joy. When those moments of love and closeness happen, kids are not as tempted to challenge and test the limits. Many confrontations can be avoided by building friendships with kids and thereby making them want to cooperate at home. It sure beats anger as a motivator of little ones!

—James C. Dobson

Training

One of your chief jobs as a mom is to train your children to behave in an acceptable way, how to respond to various situations, and to clearly communicate what is expected of them. Training is different than discipline and it must only be instigated after you have laid the foundation of nurturing in a child's life.

Train up a child in the way he should go, and when he is old he will not depart from it.
—Proverbs 22:6 NKJV

TRAINING HELPS TO COMMUNICATE DIRECTION AND EXPECTATION; IT ALSO IMPLIES THAT THERE IS AN AUTHORITY FIGURE IN CHARGE OF THESE.

One meaning of the word *train* that is found in this oft-quoted and much followed Scripture in the arena of raising children is to "put something in the mouth," such as the bit of a horse's bridle. Training, therefore, helps to communicate direction and expectation; it also implies that there is an authority figure in charge of direction and expectation. You, as the mom, know what is best for your child and it is up to you to communicate direction as well as expectation.

The word *train* has a secondary meaning: "to initiate, to inaugurate, or to place something of value." You, as the loving authority figure, should be the one who initiates the expectation of future behavior in your child's heart and awareness. Training is an offensive expectation, not defensive reaction. As a mother, you will be constantly training your progeny until the adult years when the child has left your nest.

If you have planned a trip to the library on a summer morning, training sounds like this:

"We are going to the library today and I'd like to tell you about the library. It is a quiet place where we can only walk. We are not allowed to run in the library or use our outside voices because it is not like the park. I know that you can do it. Let's practice. Can we both just use our quiet, whisper voices for two minutes?" After two minutes, tell the child, "Now, if you can just walk and not run and if you can use your indoor voice, you will get to choose three books to bring home from the library. Isn't that fun? Can you count to three?"

And then, as any competent teacher would do, you review the training several times by asking questions:

- What kind of voice can we use in the library?
- Can we run in the library? Can we jump in the library?
- How many books will you be allowed to bring home if you obey?

Children are unable to read their mother's minds nor are they able to discern situations as an adult is able to do; it will require constant communication, extra time, and abundant review as you train your children for new experiences and circumstances.

TRAINING YOUR CHILDREN FOR NEW EXPERIENCES AND CIRCUMSTANCES REQUIRES CONSTANT COMMUNICATION, EXTRA TIME, AND ABUNDANT REVIEW.

When you take your children to the dentist, the training conversation might sound something like this:

"You are going to the dentist today and it will be a brand new experience for you! It means that you are growing up! Did you know that the dentist loves to look into people's mouths? Let me see how wide you can open your mouth. Can you open as wide as a lion? As an alligator?... The dentist will hold a little mirror in his hand and a tiny silver instrument that he will use to clean your teeth. He will let you drink water from a tiny cup. You will have to hold your mouth open for a long time but I know that you can do it because you are the bravest boy that I know! While you are holding your mouth open, you can sing little songs in your head or think about your books. When it gets hard, you can tell yourself, 'I can do all things because Jesus gives me His strength.'"

The review for going to the dentist might include these questions:

+ What does the dentist like to do?

+ What will he be holding in his hand?

+ Do you have to open your eyes really wide?

+ Do you have to hold your arms in the air?

+ What will you think about when you are sitting in the big chair?

+ What songs will you sing in your mind?

+ What Bible verse can you tell yourself?

+ Can you think of another Bible verse?

When you have nurtured your child and have effectively trained them in behavior expectations, then you will be able to begin the process of disciplining your children.

> Discipline and teaching are most effective when administered in a context of a close, ongoing relationship of love.
> —Sally Clarkson

Discipline

Discipline is only effective after a child has been well trained; discipline follows the training, not the other way around. If a child has not been trained in certain behavioral expectations, then it is not fair or loving for a parent to administer discipline. As you begin to ponder and pray about what type of discipline style you will use in your family home, remind yourself often that discipline is for the purpose of making disciples.

IF A CHILD HAS NOT BEEN TRAINED IN CERTAIN BEHAVIORAL EXPECTATIONS, THEN IT IS NOT FAIR OR LOVING FOR A PARENT TO ADMINISTER DISCIPLINE.

When you have nurtured and trained a child and yet their behavior remains unacceptable, then it becomes important to discipline the child.

It is for discipline that you endure; God deals with you as with sons, for what son is there whom his father does not discipline?
—*Hebrews 12:7*

The most effective form of discipline is always birthed out of relationship not out of formula. What works for one child may not work for another. Our children are complex, developing human beings to whom we have been given oversight. As you get to know your children and model their hearts, you will learn and understand what type of discipline may work for their specific personality.

As a mother, I always wanted to mold their hearts to become submissive and unselfish through the discipline that was administered. For me, it was more about their hearts than it was about their actions. Children cannot be programmed like robots so that they will never stray. We must be gentle, patient, and kind when we are disciplining our children. Just because your child has disobeyed repeatedly does not give you, as the adult, the license to ignore the fruits of the Spirit in your life. The fruits of the Holy Spirit were given to you for fractious, challenging moments—and disciplining a child is certainly that kind of moment.

When my small children were disobedient, sometimes they didn't need discipline; they needed to be put to bed because they were overtired. During those years, I needed to think about their diet and how much sugar they had ingested. I also needed to consider whether they had been overstimulated by too much screen time or too much time with friends. I came to realize during those toddler, preschool, and even early elementary years that I had to make it easy for my children to obey by guarding their sleep, their nutrition, their entertainment, and their social lives.

WHEN SMALL CHILDREN ARE DISOBEDIENT, THEY MAY BE OVERTIRED OR OVERSTIMULATED.

I made a point, at all ages, never to raise my voice to my children unless they were in immediate danger. Why would I yell at my children when I didn't like people yelling at me? The Golden Rule doesn't cease to apply to me just because I am a mother.

Therefore, treat people the same way you want them to treat you.
—Matthew 7:12

As Christian mothers, we must apply the Word of God to our parenting style and how we discipline our children. I had a list of Scriptures that I wrote out and taped to the back of one of my kitchen cabinets that helped me to discipline out of principle and not out of emotion. The Bible is full of instructions about how we are to treat other human beings and that includes how we treat our children in those moments of discipline and frustration.

A gentle answer turns away wrath.   —Proverbs 15:1

You are your child's first taste of who God is and how God treats us. You are your child's first glimpse of the heart of the Father. You are your child's first picture of Christ. Whether they are two years old or thirty-two years old, we want our children to run to the Father in their most challenging moments of life rather than away from Him.

During my years of instructing and investing in my children's lives, I often asked myself, "How would Jesus discipline this child?" Asking myself that one compelling question often changed my paradigm in my response to inappropriate and childish behavior.

MOM NEEDS TO LET HER YOUNG CHILDREN KNOW THAT SHE LOVES THEM VERY MUCH—AND SHE'S THE BOSS.

When my children were in their toddler and preschool years and needed discipline, I knelt down so that I was on their level. I never wanted to be a giant towering over them during serious moments of correction but I desired to look into their eyes and have them look into mine. I would often take their little face in my hands and say, "Look at me. Look at Mommy's eyes." When I had their full attention, then I would say quietly, "You must obey. You do not have a choice. Mommy is the boss and you are my child. Mommy always wins. I love you very, very much but you are not allowed to act like this."

I then would have the child answer some of my questions:

+ Who always wins?

+ Are you allowed to act like this?

+ Who is the boss? Who is the child?

+ Are you in charge?

If that close and quiet action did not bring obedience, then I took the child away from the situation into another room or outside. I removed the child from the temptation, held the child on my lap or in my arms, and said, "We will wait here until you are obedient."

If that still did not work, then the little one was put to bed or not allowed to be in the situation that had instigated the disobedience. Generally, however, the seriousness of my voice, the eye-to-eye contact, and the reminder of the expectation was all that was required to solicit a child's obedience.

All of my children were classic strong-willed toddlers. But with nurturing, training, and discipleship, their hearts were turned toward obedience.

Discipline should be immediate. You should never say to a child, "You just wait until your father gets home!" The arrival of Daddy at the end of a day should be a joyful, celebratory time not a moment to be dreaded. Also, as the mother, you must establish your complete authority in dealing with disciplinary issues. I also believe that when disciplining school-age children through teenagers, the consequence should come fairly quickly after the infraction. I don't believe you should say to a teenager, "Because you were unkind to your sister, you can't go to the concert in three weeks." Instead, ask the Holy Spirit to give you a creative but timely way to discipline the erring child. For some children, no dessert is an appropriate consequence; for others, it could be no screen time, no phone, or no play dates.

NEVER WAIT FOR DADDY TO GET HOME; HIS ARRIVAL SHOULD BE A JOYFUL EXPERIENCE AND YOU HAVE COMPLETE AUTHORITY TO DEAL WITH YOUR CHILD'S BEHAVIORAL PROBLEMS IMMEDIATELY.

When you dole out a consequence for disobedience, it is important that the punishment fit the crime. Do not say something in anger that you have no intention of following through on in the days to come. Calm down, take a deep breath, walk away, and pray about the punishment. At times, when my children were ten or older, I said to them, "What do you think that an appropriate consequence would be?"

Fathers, do not provoke your children to anger, but bring them up in the discipline and instruction of the Lord.   —Ephesians 6:4

This verse makes it clear that anger should never be a component of our approach to disciplining children. However, Paul admonishes parents to "*bring them up*" using the Greek word *ektrepho*, which means "to cherish, to train, to nourish." Discipline is meant to be a nourishing experience that causes children to mature in their personhood. It begins with nurturing, moves to training, and then becomes discipleship. Discipline should never be birthed in anger, nor should it incite anger in the heart of a child. This does not mean that a child will enjoy discipline, but it does mean that when the discipline is given by a parent who has loved the child completely and communicated an expectation of behavior thoroughly, discipleship has taken place.

DISCIPLINE SHOULD NEVER BE BIRTHED IN ANGER, NOR SHOULD IT INCITE ANGER IN THE HEART OF A CHILD.

A child should never be disciplined for childish behavior like spilling milk or being afraid of a situation. Discipline should only be given for willful disobedience.

As the mother of five strong-willed, opinionated, creative children, I can assure you that there were intense moments from time to time in our home, but we tried to banish the word *angry* from our emotional pantry. *Angry* should never be used to describe who you are as a parent or how a little one feels about you.

For the moment, all discipline seems not to be pleasant, but painful; yet to those who have been trained by it, afterward it yields the peaceful fruit of righteousness. —Hebrews 12:11

The goal of a mother in doling out discipline is to obtain the peaceful fruit of righteousness. I always tried to be a mother who was easy to obey; I didn't want to be so exacting and legalistic that my children had a hard time living in my home.

As Craig and I were raising our children, we often said, "It's more fun to obey than it is to disobey!"

Finally, don't underestimate the power of taking the time to pray for a disobedient child. I prayed over my babies who refused to sleep, I prayed over my two-year-olds who were throwing tantrums, I prayed over eight-year-olds who were selfish and unkind, and I prayed over teenagers who were out too late. Your prayers may be the redirection and the strength-giving discipline that your child needs.

The "Rod"

Nearly everyone has an opinion about spanking and corporal punishment. I, too, have an opinion that is based upon Scripture, upon years of studying philosophies of parenting, and by listening to people whom I deeply respect.

I believe in discipline and I believe that the parent should be the authority figure. My children knew, beyond a shadow of a doubt, that Craig and I were in charge and that they must obey completely, immediately, and with a happy heart. Craig and I were diligent in disciplining our children with consistency and with expected obedience.

I'd like to humbly and quietly tell you that Craig and I did spank our children. We didn't spank them often, but when all other approaches had failed, we were known to use an instrument other than our hands on the backside of a child.

 JESUS WOULD NOT SPANK A CHILD AND NEITHER SHOULD WE.

However, I will also humbly and gently say that if I had to do it all over again, I would not spank. When I ask myself the question, "How would Jesus discipline a child?" I never answer it by saying, "He would hit a little one."

Evangelical Christianity has chiefly based its belief in spanking on this Scripture:

He who withholds his rod hates his son, but he who loves him disciplines him diligently. —Proverbs 13:24

As an older mother—and hopefully a mentor to you by now—I want to assure you that the phrase, "Spare the rod, spoil the child" does not come from Scripture but from a poem written in 1662 by Samuel Butler.

In order to understand the heart and instruction of this Proverb, we must understand that in ancient times, the rod was used by shepherds to guide and guard their sheep.

The word *rod* in the Hebrew is *sebet* and it occurs 190 times in the Old Testament. Depending upon the context of the passage, it can mean several different things:

+ Most frequently, it means *tribe*, which is a totally different usage than that in Proverbs 13:24, so we can remove this meaning from the discussion.

+ Secondly, it means a rod made of metal or wood that was used for beating seed.

+ At times, it's translated as a weapon such as *javelin* or *club* in the context of battle, war, or fighting an enemy.

+ It can also mean scepter, which would be symbolic of authority or rulership, and was used contextually in a ceremonial sense.

+ And finally, it means shepherd's rod; also described as a *staff* or a *crook*.

As I have studied the word *sebet* over the years, I believe the best understanding of Proverbs 13:24 is that of the shepherd's rod. The verse that's been used to support disciplining a child by spanking simply does not agree with the rest of Scripture.

Shepherding is about the care, oversight, and leading of a flock of sheep from one location to another. In the New Testament, Jesus refers to Himself as "the Good Shepherd" and we are called to be the image bearers of Christ.

The rod was always in the shepherd's hand as he closely led the sheep away from trouble and harm. He walked in front of the sheep so that their gaze was always on him and his rod. The shepherd clearly led the way for the sheep to follow. You, as the parent, need to lead the way for your children at all times. You need to model kind speech, unselfish choices, and godly behavior so that your children will follow your example.

YOU NEED TO MODEL KIND SPEECH, UNSELFISH CHOICES, AND GODLY BEHAVIOR SO THAT YOUR CHILDREN WILL FOLLOW YOUR EXAMPLE.

Sheep, like children, are easily distracted by things seen in their peripheral vision; the shepherd used his rod to guide them back on the right path. Even when his sheep were wandering, a good, loving shepherd would not strike them. Doing so would only slow the animal down and make it afraid of the shepherd. If you, as the shepherd of your children, are distracted by social media, entertainment, spending rather than saving, and emotional outrage, your children will not know how to make good decisions in life. Stick to the boundaries that you have set for your family.

The shepherd also carried a staff with a hook or crook on one end that he used when necessary to pull a sheep away from extreme danger. There will be times when you, too, will need to pull your children away from danger.

The shepherd used his rod as a weapon against predators such as wolves and mountain lions that threatened his dearly loved flock. The rod could also help a shepherd count his sheep to make sure that none were lost or had wandered away.

Finally, the rod was used as an extension of the shepherd's hand to lift and carry a sheep or examine its skin for injury. A skilled shepherd could take his rod, part the sheep's thick wool, and carefully inspect the beloved animal's skin to look for signs of disease, wounds, or burrowing insects.

Sheep need a shepherd to lead them; they need a shepherd who will keep them away from danger, protect them from predators, and take them to pleasant pastures in which to graze.

Just like sheep, children need to be led, guided, and protected by their parents. But like the Good Shepherd, the rod should only be used to point the way, to nurture, to protect, and to influence.

Your rod and Your staff, they comfort me. —Psalm 23:4

When we are fearful and worried all the time, we are living as if we don't believe that we have a strong and able Shepherd who is tenderhearted toward us, who only leads us to good places, who protects us and lovingly watches over us. —Joseph Prince

9

The Library

One who walks with wise people will be wise. —Proverbs 13:20

I have always longed to have a library in my home. Just imagine: a room solely dedicated to the housing of exquisite books from floor to ceiling. A library is a place of quiet repose, instant learning, and vivid imagination. I do believe that every time I would enter that exciting yet quiet room of my imagination, my heart would begin to beat faster with the adrenaline of anticipation.

I have never lived in a home grand enough to have one room dedicated solely to books and so, understandably, my books have been scattered throughout the entire house. In the kitchen, you will find cookbooks, perhaps a storybook or two for the grandchildren, and also a tossed-aside copy of a book that has only been half-read. In the living room, there is likely to be a picture book on the coffee table, along with a Bible commentary and a well-read copy of *Little Women* or *Tom Sawyer*. On my bedroom table lies a stack of books that I simply *must* read; it's threatening to topple over as it grows...and grows.

I'm sure you have discerned by now that I love books. I love everything about a good, wholesome, classic, intriguing, challenging read. I love the way that the pages feel as I turn them and the smell of the ink upon the page.

Books are quiet companions that often shout into the caverns of my soul. A book may only weigh a pound or two but its gravity creates a heavy weight of experience, knowledge, and hope.

In the beginning was the Word, and the Word was with God, and the Word was God. —John 1:1

Certainly, if the Bible describes God as *"the Word,"* then it stands to reason that words are important in His kingdom. If you desire to give your children a head start in their education and a solid foundation for future academia, then you, as the mother, must have an awe-inspiring library in your heart. You must read aloud to your children and give them books for their birthdays, Christmas, and other special occasions. You must turn off your screens and read the tales and adventures of childhood to the impressionable crew that you have been given.

Show me a family of readers and I will show you the people who move the world. —Napoleon Bonaparte

A Family that Reads Together

I have always been a book girl, often referring to myself as a "read-aholic," and have dispensed that love of reading to every single one of my five children. You can travel through time on the pages of a good book, you can live on another continent through the transportation of a favorite book, and you can become anyone you want to be simply by reading a book!

A room without books is like a body without a soul. —Cicero

Your children will learn to love what you tenderly present to them; if your children have been given the priceless gift of a mother who reads, you are well on your way to developing voracious readers as well. The habit and hobby of ingesting literature is able to strengthen your walk with the Lord and develop the faith of your children.

Words have power to change, to enlarge, and to teach. The books that are in your family home should become some of your children's best friends as they grow up. If you love books, it is likely that your children will as well. The stories that your children read will expand their understanding and their love of the world and its cultures. Books can meet children at any age and help them to traverse the challenges of life. The characters in children's books and classic literature can spur on healthy conversation in the library of your heart. You will discover heroes and heroines on the pages of a well-written book, you will be able to discuss villains and what motivated their poor choices, and you will be able to identify your child's affinity for calling and for purpose.

BOOKS CAN MEET CHILDREN AT ANY AGE AND HELP THEM TO TRAVERSE THE CHALLENGES OF LIFE.

When a mom encourages a child to read, it also expands their vocabulary in an engaging and even exciting manner. When a child reads, they learn of history, science, music, art, and nature all while snuggled on the family room couch!

Often, when dealing with a difficult family situation such as deceit, selfishness, or laziness, I would read a book out loud that addressed that particular challenge. We could then discuss the virtue that we all needed to embrace in the family and thus spur one another on to love and good deeds.

Just before his tenth birthday, one of my children struggled with telling the truth. He had a tendency to exaggerate and seem more knowledgeable than he actually was on a topic. This beloved son and his dad began to study verses in Scripture that addressed the importance of speaking the truth and even memorized many of the verses together, father and son. I assigned books to this lively, energetic boy that told stories about people who did not tell the truth and the consequences they then faced. I also required him to read stories about heroes and heroines who chose to tell the truth even when it was hard. We diligently combined biographies, the Word of God, and literature to help our son learn the value of honesty and integrity. He has grown into quite the godly man!

There is no friend as loyal as a book.   —Ernest Hemingway

The Journey into Literature

My journey into the world of literature began after my first week of second grade. That Friday afternoon, my teacher handed me a copy of *Little House in the Big Woods*. I had read the entire book by Monday, when she had the second book in the series ready for me.

After devouring the *Little House* series, I then graduated to *Betsy-Tacy and Tib*, *All of a Kind Family*, and *Caddie Woodlawn*. In not much time at all, I was reading *Little Women*.

By the time I completed the fifth grade in the elementary school building, I had read every book in its library. I had read sports stories, biographies, the *You Were There* series, and fiction. In the sixth grade, the elementary school librarian took me to the high school library once a week to borrow books so that my reading would not be stifled.

THE INFLUENCE THAT AN ADULT IS ABLE TO HAVE ON A CHILD'S LIFE WILL RIPPLE THROUGH THE YEARS AND FORM THEIR VERY CHARACTER.

I tell you this not to boast but to let you know that my parents and my teachers applauded this novice addiction in my life. They encouraged my love of words and my desire to read. The influence that an adult is able to have on a child's life will ripple through the years and form their very character. You are that adult in your child's life, mom! Cultivating a fragrant and healthy love of reading will add hours and even years of enjoyment to each of your children's lives.

Books are the quietest and most constant of friends; they are the most accessible and wisest of counselors, and the most patient of teachers.
                                        —Charles W. Eliot

To Read or Not to Read

If you have a child who does not enjoy reading, begin by reading out loud to this child. Use accents, hand motions, and different voices as you read. Make the book come alive with enthusiasm and drama. Select books that pique the child's interest or speak to his or her hobbies. If you have a little boy who loves alligators, then read every age-appropriate book you can find about alligators. If your daughter is enamored by the world of ballet, then research books that will encourage this healthy interest in her life.

One of my sons was not a good reader and did not enjoy reading during his elementary school years. It was a chore and a struggle for him, not the delight that it was for the rest of us. We had many tears of frustration over his lack of desire to read. I rewarded him with treats and extra playtime when he successfully read a book and could discuss it with me.

My dear Aunt Marianne, who had taught sixth grade for forty years, encouraged me to allow him to read comic books, the back of cereal boxes, and books that were below his grade level so that he would feel competent.

When he hit the middle school years, he received a portable CD player for Christmas. Being an auditory learner, this diligent child then began to discover the wonder of listening to books on CD. He listened to the works of C. S. Lewis, J. R. R. Tolkien, and George McDonald. Today, as a man in his thirties, he is the most voracious reader of all of my children. He always has his nose in a book…or in his e-reader!

If your children are anything at all like my children were or my grandchildren are today, they are always begging for screen time. Rather than staying in a constant state of frustration with my children, I decided that I would barter with them. For every minute that they practiced a musical instrument or read a book, they would receive thirty seconds of screen time. So, if they read for an hour, they could then be on the computer or play a video game for thirty minutes. We kept track of these bartered hours on a chart on the refrigerator and I had to sign off on their deposit in their screen time account.

Fill your house with stacks of books, in all the crannies and all the nooks.

—Dr. Seuss

A Book Party

Often, on snowy winter nights or rainy afternoons, when the children were preschoolers or in the early elementary years, I would announce, "It's time for a book party!" They knew what that meant and scrambled to do their part. I placed a laundry basket in the middle of the living room floor and each child was allowed to place five favorite books in the basket.

As they were choosing their books, I was creating the much anticipated *snack plates* for each child. These plates might hold grapes, crackers, raisins, bananas, popcorn, apple slices, or pieces of cheese. There might be a peanut butter and jelly sandwich cut into fun shapes with cookie cutters. We would either snuggle on our well-worn couch or spread a picnic blanket on the carpet and the book party would begin!

I read out loud for hours until every book in the basket had been completely relished from cover to cover. Often, we took a hot chocolate break in the middle of our party just to stretch our limbs and give my vocal cords a break.

> Reading should not be presented to children as a chore or a duty.
> It should be offered as a gift.　　　　　　　—Kate DiCamillo

Adventures in Books...and Laundry

Oh, the mountains of laundry that appeared at my house on a daily basis! It was easy for me to throw a load of laundry into my irritable washing machine and then to transfer it, or have a child transfer it, to the moody dryer; I could handle the laundry that magically appeared on every bedroom floor in the family home. However, the conundrum of it all was to keep up with the incessant, constant, and perpetual folding.

If one of my sons needed clean underwear, he often had to run into the family room with a towel wrapped around his waist in order to paw through Mt. Laundry and unearth the underwear that had been washed and dried three days earlier. And who could ever find matching socks in that pile? Socks hid amid the kitchen towels, little girls' skirts, and football uniforms.

Eventually, I knew that I needed the children to help me conquer Mt. Laundry, so I threw a clothes folding party in my bedroom twice a week. All of the clean laundry was piled on the bed as I corralled every breathing member of the family to join me in preparation for family bonding time. The first time I planned this party, there were some vigorous complaints and just a tad bit of whining.

AS THE CHILDREN TACKLED MT. LAUNDRY, WE LISTENED TO THEIR FAVORITE STORY FROM *ADVENTURES IN ODYSSEY* ON MY CD PLAYER.

As the children walked into the bedroom for our first clothes folding party, they heard the strains of their favorite story from *Adventures in Odyssey* playing on my CD player. As they tackled the mountain and it began to dissipate before our very eyes, all of the children, ages three through sixteen, listened to another tale from Whit's End. Somehow, when their imaginations were gathered with the gang in Odyssey, regardless of their age, they were able to unconsciously fold towels, T-shirts, and pants, as well as match most of the clean socks.

The clothes were folded and put away easily, almost instinctively, because their imaginations were far, far away. Thank you, Mr. Whittaker!

A children's story that can only be enjoyed by children is not a good children's story in the slightest.   —C. S. Lewis

Ages and Stages

One of your most consuming jobs as the librarian of the family home is to know which books your children should be reading and what particular books should be read to them at different ages and stages. You should always have at hand a new book for a child to meander through, whether it is from the library, a thrift shop, borrowed from a friend, or a new book tucked away for a particular moment. Books should be doled out to your family just as healthy meals are given three times a day. There should never be a dearth of books in your family home, nor should the words, "Mom, I have nothing to read" ever be spoken.

And, oh! Let me just tell you that I can't wait to give you an amazing gift that I have prepared just for you! I can't wait to share with you the titles and the authors that have shaped my life as well as the lives of my children and now my grandchildren in a myriad of ways. In Appendix A, you may discover the greatest treasure of this entire book—list upon list of various books for different ages and stages, with different purposes in mind. As I have remembered, studied, and researched what titles and authors to share with you in the library of your heart, I have been like a mother on Christmas Eve! I cannot wait for you to open the cover of each book and discover a new friend, a new joy, and a new reason to believe again. And let me just say ahead of time, "You're welcome!"

> Books are good company, in sad times and happy times, for books are people—people who have managed to stay alive by hiding between the covers of a book.   —E. B. White

10

The Music Room

That my soul may sing praise to You and not be silent. LORD *my God, I will give thanks to You forever.* —Psalm 30:12

Take a deep breath, close your eyes, and listen for the music. Allow the music of motherhood to fill your very soul. There are other sounds that will try to distract you from the symphony that belongs solely to you and to those who create the melodies with you. The cacophony of busyness, others' expectations, daily frustrations, and the demands of life will converge to drown out the song of your heart but please do not allow those things to keep you from the theme that you were meant to sing as a mother.

The music room of motherhood is so expansive and so thrilling that I can't wait for you to join me in this happy yet holy place. As the mother of your family and the one who has been charged with creating the atmosphere of your home, you are called to fill it with song. What a glorious assignment!

You are the one who will write the splendid lyrics that describe the childhood of those who live in your home. You will be the one who cheerfully and purposefully composes the lavish melodies that will never leave the hearts of your flock. You, dear mom, are the leading conductor of the happy sounds of life that take place in your home.

One of the most meaningful and blessed assignments given to a mother is to be a songstress, a woman who fills her home and her heart with the strength of a song. Let a song fill your heart every morning when you get out of bed and rub the sleep out of your eyes. Begin to sing a song of faith while you brush your teeth and when you (hopefully!) have the time to comb your hair!

ONE OF THE MOST MEANINGFUL AND BLESSED ASSIGNMENTS GIVEN TO A MOTHER IS TO BE A WOMAN WHO FILLS HER HOME AND HER HEART WITH THE STRENGTH OF A SONG.

While you are nursing your baby, sing a sweet lullaby and a worship chorus. When the toddlers are cranky, change the atmosphere with a rousing rendition of "The Itsy Bitsy Spider" and "Do-Re-Mi" from *The Sound of Music*.

Perhaps by this time you are tempted to roll your eyes at me and say in your most respectful yet condescending voice, "But, Carol, I can't carry a tune! There is no way that I can fill my home with music!"

Oh, sweet mother! Let me assure you that you don't need to have a degree from The Juilliard School or the voice of Julie Andrews in order to fill your home with song. If you can whistle, you have a song in your heart. If you can play the radio, a CD, or an online music app, you can supply your home with the melodies of life.

The music that you will sing over your children will be both auditory and silent. Some of the music will come from within you while some of it will be purposefully gathered and played while you live your days in the house that you call home.

Music is life itself.

—Louis Armstrong

A Mother Who Sings

I have probably said this to you before, but allow me the delight of repeating myself: your home should be the happiest home on your street simply because you are the mom and Jesus lives there with you! Your children should never wonder if their mom has a song in her heart or not; your song should be a perpetual part of your personality and your spirit. There should be no event, no challenge, or no circumstance that robs you of the music of the soul.

Mothers who choose to sing their crying little ones to sleep communicate peace and unconditional love. Mothers who choose to sing their way through a two-year-old meltdown discover that two-year-olds don't rule the world. When you sing, dear mama, the entire family will join in your song. If you choose not to sing, you will be creating a vacuum that sucks away the joy of daily living.

LITTLE DITTIES HELP YOUR CHILDREN MAKE IT THROUGH ORDINARY TASKS, MUNDANE DAYS, AND AVERAGE EVENTS.

I am known for writing songs for children. Nothing very impressive, I assure you, just little ditties that helped us make it through ordinary tasks, mundane days, and average events. Would you like to read some of my outstanding lyrics? Sung to the tune of "Twinkle, Twinkle, Little Star" is this gem:

"Tinkle, tinkle, little Matt. In your diaper there's a splat. Sometimes when my folks change me, on their nose goes my pee-pee!"

Or then there is this McLeod classic song that is sure to help a two-year-old giggle his or her way right out of a tantrum:

Bonk-Bonk-Doodle-Ooot
Bonk-Bonk-Doodle-Ooot
Because you're little, you're little
You're tiny to your mommy.
You're little, you're little
And you're not growing up.
I love you, I love you, every single day.
You're my little baby girl (boy) just all along life's way
Doodle-Ooot
Bonk-Bonk – Doodle-Ooot
But then you're growing, you're growing

And you are getting bigger.
You're braver, you're stronger and you are getting taller
I love you, I love you, every single day.
You're my precious growing girl (boy) just all along life's way.
Doodle-Ooot
Bonk-Bonk-Doodle-Ooot

There will be days when the loudest music played in your home is the silent music of your heart. You must choose a song of joy when your child's world has fallen apart, when the bills are not paid, and when you are walking through emotional pain. The song of a mother's heart is able to heal the fiercest distress and mend the most aching agony. You must never underestimate the power of your song; I can assure you that it will live vibrantly beyond the years that you have been singing it to those under your roof. The song of a mother's heart will echo through your child's life into adulthood.

THE SONG OF A MOTHER'S HEART IS ABLE TO HEAL THE FIERCEST DISTRESS AND MEND THE MOST ACHING AGONY.

My Irish, godly grandmother, who spent her childhood in a Catholic orphanage, raised her babies during the Great Depression. They remember vividly that as she rocked them, she sang, to the tune of "Come Thou Fount of Every Blessing," the repetitive lyrics:

Mama's baby, Mama's baby, Mama's baby, baby boy (girl)
Mama's baby, Mama's baby, Mama's baby, baby boy (girl)

When my grandmother's children grew up, they sang the same tune with the same lyrics to their children, who sang it to their children, who are now singing it through every long night to their children. What a rare gift to give to the generations to come—the gift of a family song!

Some days there won't be a song in your heart. Sing anyway.
—Emory Austin

October 1

As I held my newborn babies in my arms in the delivery room, I could never hold back the song in my heart. The first song that I sang to all five of my babies was "Jesus Loves Me" because before they knew another thing about life on earth, I wanted each one of them to know that they were loved by Jesus. The second song that I sang to them when they were just minutes old was "I'll Be Home for Christmas" because I wanted to remind them that home is where they belonged for every Christmas of their lives! "I'll Be Home for Christmas" became the McLeod family theme song and to this day serves as a reminder that all hearts come home for Christmas.

I am a bona fide, diagnosed "Christmas-aholic"! I love everything about the holiday season; I love the gifts, the food, the joy, the cards, and the decorations. I am addicted to it all! However, the aspect of Christmas that I love the most is the music that is timeless, triumphant, and jubilant.

When I was in college, I had a roommate who felt the same way that I did about the melodies of Christmas. We made an audacious declaration that the first official day of the Christmas music season was October 1. We believed that Christmas music is just too spectacular to listen to only one short month of the calendar year. It must be savored throughout the months of October, November, and December.

On October 1, we decorated our room with every Christmas decoration we had in our possession and lit a pine-scented candle that filled the room with the seasonal aroma. We put up signs in our dormitory hallway, inviting everyone to a celebration in our room that evening. We made Christmas cookies and hot chocolate for our unsuspecting friends; as they gathered around the door, the sounds of Christmas came wafting out. It was only October 1, but Christmas had started in our hallway and in our hearts.

ON OCTOBER 1, THE FIRST SONG OF THE DAY WAS ALWAYS "I'LL BE HOME FOR CHRISTMAS."

The tradition has continued throughout all of my years of mothering. On October 1, the first song of the day was always "I'll Be Home for Christmas."

The Christmas candles were lit and I served peppermint ice cream for dessert that evening. As the years of childhood flew by, my children loved October 1 so much that they wanted to invite their friends to our celebration. Our home on that sparkling day was filled to overflowing with church families, high school friends, and neighbors. We sang Christmas carols, drank hot chocolate, and enjoyed the power of music.

To this day, I call my children early on the morning of October 1 and play the strains of "I'll Be Home for Christmas" across the miles to them. I hope that my children will always remember that their mom had a song of Christmas in her heart every day of the year.

Someone once said, "It's never too early for Christmas music." I wish I had said it first!

Every Day All Day

If you are at home on any given day at any random hour, that is a signal that music should be playing. Although some experts believe that Mozart enhances your baby's intelligence, I can tell you that *all* good music is beneficial in your home. Your home should be the first place where your children are introduced to Broadway show tunes and patriotic music; if you play classical music early enough, they will actually learn to enjoy it. Perhaps it would be fun to invite your parents over and then savor an evening of oldies that they listened to when they were young. Gather in the family room and sing along with the great hymns of the faith that thousands have sung before you. I know many young mothers who allow their children to fall asleep while listening to contemporary worship music.

It is important to have music playing in the background continually, but it is even more important to have your children interact with the music that is being played. With a baby, you can move his or her hands and legs to the beat of the music. You can begin a conversation with a toddler by saying, "This song makes me feel like marching. How does it make you feel?"

I loved spending time with my children just singing the songs of childhood! When they were young, we sang simple songs with repetitive lyrics and melodies. Hand clapping was encouraged as we entered into the wonderful world of music together. When they learned the melodies, I could then ask questions such as:

+ Does the next note go up or down?

+ Is this a loud song or a quiet song?

+ Is this a fast song or a slow song?

And, dear mama, in the music room of your heart, you must make time to dance with your children! The ability to discover the beat of music and then to move to it is foundational to their future musical abilities. A family who dances together is also a family who knows how to sing together, to laugh together, and to turn an ordinary afternoon into a party. You can begin to dance with your baby while it is just a newborn and continue to dance until they go away to college.

A FAMILY WHO DANCES TOGETHER IS ALSO A FAMILY WHO KNOWS HOW TO SING TOGETHER, TO LAUGH TOGETHER, AND TO TURN AN ORDINARY AFTERNOON INTO A PARTY.

And finally, discover the joy of making music together. If you play the piano, gather the family around and sing at the top of your lungs. As your children learn to play the piano, choose easy duets that you can play together. The shared joy of making music together will bind your hearts together in a way that little else can do. If you don't play the piano, buy other instruments that the entire family can enjoy, such as drums, a recorder, a keyboard, a guitar, or an autoharp.

Invite your family into the music room of your heart. If music is important to you, you can transfer that same love to the little ones who share your home. As you allow the song in your heart to be demonstrated and heard, they, too, will begin to celebrate the wonder of music.

A bird doesn't sing because it has an answer. It sings because it has a song.
—Maya Angelou

An Eclectic Selection

Here's a practical discipline that you must embrace in the music room of your heart: make sure that you are exposing your children to different types and styles of music. In order to accomplish this, let me share the list that I used in order to be aware of the styles of music to which we were listening around the calendar year:

- January: classical composers such as Mozart, Beethoven, and Bach
- February: love songs by composers such as Irving Berlin, George Gershwin, and Cole Porter
- March: Broadway show tunes
- April: pieces by twentieth-century composers such as Béla Bartok, Benjamin Britten, and Charles Ives
- May: waltzes by composers such as Strauss, Chopin, and Tchaikovsky
- June: music from World War I and World War II such as "Over There" and "Boogie Woogie Bugle Boy"
- July: patriotic tunes
- August: oldies from the 1940s, '50s, and '60s
- September: scores from movies
- October: jazz, the blues and Christmas music
- November: great hymns of the faith and Christmas music
- December: Christmas music

Of course, you are not limited to my list but can create your own list based upon the musical genres that are meaningful to you. Whatever you do, have fun with music! Don't make it into a drudgery but invite your children, at every age, to sing along with Mom.

The earth has music for those who listen.

—William Shakespeare

The Soundtrack of My Heart

Shortly after our fifth child, Joni Rebecca, was born, I was sitting in church waiting for the service to begin. On that particular day, we were having a special singer whom I had admired from afar for many years. I couldn't wait to hear her voice and just rest in the resonance and musicality that was sure to be there. Our two older sons were sitting in the row in front of me with their high school friends; I had a lively six-year-old boy on one side of me, a dependent three-year-old girl on the other side of me, and a newborn baby in my arms. I was still wearing maternity clothes because I had nothing that fit me. I noticed spit-up on my shoulders and I wondered when the last time was that I had worn makeup to church.

The guest artist was introduced and from the very first note, I was spell-bound by her talent, her devotion, and her stage presence. It wasn't long into the concert, however, when the tears began to roll down my cheeks. No matter how desperately I tried not to cry, the tears turned into shoulder-shaking sobs and I couldn't control my emotions. I felt unimportant in that moment, as if my life were inconsequential. When I compared my little life to this singer's amazing platform, my self-esteem and my hope for influence were ripped away from me. I wondered what had happened to the girl I used to be, the one with big dreams and grand potential. Would my life always be defined by the unmade beds, the mountains of laundry, and the accumulated weight of five pregnancies?

In that life-changing moment, I heard the soft whisper of the Holy Spirit say to me, "Carol, your magnum opus is your call to motherhood. You are writing a symphony in the heart of each child. They will sing their songs for decades to come simply because you were their mom."

I was able to wipe my tears away—grateful that I had not had time to put on any mascara that morning—and turn my heart toward the lovely strains of music that were filling the sanctuary around me. When the final note of the final song had been sung, the singer's concert had been completed...but mine had just begun. I knew that the song of my life was every bit as beautiful as the voice of that award-winning artist. That unforgettable morning in church helped me realize that the music I would share with the little people under my watch would echo for generations to come.

Music is the soundtrack of your life.   —Dick Clark

11

The Family Room

But the godly are happy; they rejoice before God and are overcome with joy.

—Psalm 68:3 NET

Have you decided to *be* a family? Have you determined that you will indeed celebrate the personalities and preferences of those amazing individuals who live under the same roof? So much about *us* is up to us!

As the mother of the unique brood that you have been given, you are the keeper of the keys of your family. To a large degree, you hold the exclusive key to the happiness that your family will experience, the contentment that is shared, and the bonding that is cultivated. Every door of fun, traditions, and celebration that you unlock, as the keeper of the keys, is a door that is now open for the purpose of apprehending a happier family life involving more contented individuals. A mother is the one person who can decide to honor the miracle that is named *family*. She knows that happiness happens in the family room of her heart.

When your children are mere infants, you will gather them in your arms. As they grow into toddlers, they will be assembled around your knees. As they become lively and precocious school-age children, they will likely congregate around the kitchen table or in the family room. And then, when they leave the nest, the traditions that you established, the games that you played, and the fun that defined your brood will linger still in the hallways of your heart.

 WHEN A CHILD THINKS OF HOME, HE OR SHE SHOULD THINK OF SAFETY, FAITH, STABILITY, AND FUN.

Children should experience their first truly wonderful memories in the family home. When a child thinks of home, he or she should think of safety, faith, stability, and fun. The family room is a place of laughter and raucous games; it is marked by creativity, innovation, and traditions. The family room just may be the very best place of a mother's heart because this is where unity is perfected and where identity is established. We are a family because of the happenings in the family room.

As we enter the family room of your heart, sweet mama, remind yourself often that you are the keeper of the keys of every activity that joins your family in an unspoken yet powerful camaraderie. You hold the keys. Every day lived together as a family can be a red-letter day just because the mom decided to make it so.

Tradition! Tradition!

One of the greatest and longest lasting gifts that you can give to your children is the gift of family traditions. Traditions are likely to become the glue that ties the children's hearts together as they grow into adults. Developing and maintaining traditions is chiefly the job of the mother, who is the keeper of the keys to the family room.

Traditions are the sweetest and most long-lasting ways of declaring, "We are a family! We belong together! We love doing life together!" Our lives are richer for the shared rituals that are worthy of marking and sustaining. A tradition is a family holiday without a name; it is a calendar-worthy event that claims no red-letter day on any other calendar but the one that hangs in your home.

The traditions that you establish in your home today are the memories that your children will embrace tomorrow. Traditions require forethought and focused intentionality so that they leave lasting footprints on your child's heart. Meg Cox, the author of *The Book of New Family Traditions*, defines these beloved family rituals as "any activity you purposefully repeat together as a family that includes heightened attentiveness and something extra that lifts it above the ordinary ruts."[4] Family traditions create the very fabric of the life that happens within your home.

TRADITIONS ARE ABLE TO SHAPE A CHILD'S PERSONAL IDENTITY SIMPLY BECAUSE THEY TELL A STORY ABOUT ONE'S FAMILY.

Traditions are able to shape a child's personal identity simply because they tell a story about one's family. These beloved habits can also strengthen the family bond. Research has discovered that families who value traditions as part of the family culture develop stronger unity than families who don't participate in or enjoy family customs.[5]

Traditions also supply relief from the busy world that children often live in; family habits can offer a constant that becomes a shelter from the outside world. Traditions are able to provide both comfort and security to children who are going through change in their lives, such as relocation to a new home, the birth of a baby, or the death of a grandparent.

One of the aspects of family traditions that I cherished the most was the opportunity to teach family values. The tradition of praying around the dinner table or before bedtime communicates the fact that our family believes in prayer. The tradition of reading bedtime stories embraces the esteem that we hold for reading and literature. When there is music playing in the home during the morning hours, it reenforces the joy that music offers to family life.

Traditions can also serve as a lovely way to connect the generations when you include grandparents, cousins, or aunts and uncles in movie night, a scavenger hunt, or memory night. Sociologists have found that children who have

4. Meg Cox, *The Book of New Family Traditions: How to Create Great Rituals for Holidays and Everyday* (Philadelphia, PA: Running Press, 2003).
5. Brett and Kate McKay, "Creating a Positive Family Culture: The Importance of Establishing Family Traditions," *The Art of Manliness*, September 19, 2020 (www.artofmanliness.com/articles/creating-a-positive-family-culture-the-importance-of-establishing-family-traditions).

a high level of grandparent involvement have fewer emotional and behavioral problems. Also, regular involvement by the grandparents in a family's life is associated with lower maternal stress and higher involvement from the father.[6]

And finally, traditions create lasting memories that will linger long beyond the years of childhood. Sweet and genuine memories will help to develop an emotionally healthy and stable adult.

Birthday Traditions

Sometimes, traditions are planned and well-crafted; at other times, traditions are born out of sheer desperation. Such is the birthday tradition that we began nearly forty years ago when our oldest sons were only two and four years old. On a cold, winter morning, when my bank account was low but my boys deserved a birthday celebration, I discovered that necessity truly is the mother of invention.

Matthew and Christopher were born during the month of January just two years apart. Their birthdays were only two days apart. Trying to live on a pastor's salary was challenging enough year-round but it was especially difficult during the holiday season. We never had time to recover from the expenses of Christmas before it was time to celebrate these two small men whom we loved more than life itself!

On the evening before Christopher's birthday, I knew that I wasn't able to buy him a new train set, a teddy bear, or even a small car. We had the ingredients for a birthday cake for both boys but that was the limit of our budget during that frigid season. I looked at what I had and what I could possibly make for my excited sons. I had construction paper, glitter, markers, and tape. Now, believe me when I say that I am not a creative genius but with love in my heart laced with fortitude, I began to make birthday signs for my little men:

Chris is 2!
Matt is 4!
Happy Birthday!
You make me smile!
Jesus loves you!

---

6. Ibid.

The signs were simple but sparkly; they were written with love and placed all over our small home. There was a birthday sign on every kitchen cabinet, on the bathroom mirror, and on each window in the house. Birthday signs were hanging from light fixtures, attached to the television screen, and taped on their bedroom ceilings.

The birthday signs continued through the years and their messages grew with our family:

Mom, Dad, Matt, Chris, Jordan and Joy all love Joni Becca!
September 2, 1988
Carolyn Joy-Belle McLeod is 10!

As the years passed, we became more creative with the signs and listed their favorite TV shows, favorite books, and best friends. It was an inexpensive but valuable way to show our love for our children on their birthday and involve the entire family. The wonder of it all is that although my children are grown and gone with families of their own, the tradition continues. They now make birthday signs for their families and even their children are beginning to participate in this meaningful yet simple birthday tradition.

Another birthday tradition that filled our home with security and love was the practice of giving a *word gift* to each person on their birthday. Each family member came to the dinner table prepared to say one kind thing about the person whose birthday we were celebrating. It was a gift of love that meant more than anything tangible that had been wrapped in bright colored paper and tied with a fetching bow.

After the word gifts had been given by every person to the birthday child, then we laid hands on the person who was being celebrated and prayed for him or her. At the close of the day, as the birthday child was being tucked into bed, I would lovingly tell the story of the day of his or her birth, often through sobs and tears. It became a treasured tradition to remember these birth days that had changed my life forever.

Dinner Time

In our achievement-driven society, dinnertime is often the only time that a family truly sits down just to be together and enjoy each other's company.

The bonding that takes place at dinnertime over a shared meal should always be peppered with interesting conversation. It is of vital importance for all members of your family to sit down once a day to enjoy a nutritious meal, look into each other's eyes, and hear one another's hearts.

If you, as the mom, will put just a little effort into making the meal a time of celebration and sweet sharing, you will find that it goes a long way toward the goal of uniting the hearts of your family together in love.

Every meal should begin with prayer. Even if the entire family is not together, the ones who are gathered should always remember to pray together for God's blessing on the food and to thank Him for His provision. At our family table, we took turns praying so that everyone had a chance to lead the family in prayer. We didn't allow anyone to skip his or her turn but encouraged each one to be a contributor to the family tradition of prayer.

Although it wasn't a daily achievement, there were many dinners during the week at which I lit a candle or two, used real cloth napkins and even hauled out the fine china. It's true that some nights we ate on paper plates with plastic utensils; how we all loved those dinners that were gloriously easy to clean up! However, I also knew that my children needed to be taught manners and experience the peace that is able to envelope a meal when beauty is expressed by place settings, classical music, and even fresh flowers. When a child realizes that a meal has been thoughtfully designed and creatively presented by their mother, his or her heart opens to the wonder of family fellowship and shared unity.

WHEN MOM THOUGHTFULLY DESIGNS AND CREATIVELY PRESENTS A MEAL, A CHILD'S HEART OPENS TO THE WONDER OF FAMILY FELLOWSHIP AND SHARED UNITY.

We did not allow disagreements to take place at the dinner table. If a verbal scuffle broke out between two of the children over a family meal, they were both quickly sent away from the dinner table and could only come back when they had forgiven each other and were ready to be kind and encouraging.

The purpose of the dinner hour was to be one of shared interests, listening hearts, and captivating conversation; I was the one who held the keys to opening the door to a fruitful and nutritious exchange.

Craig and I often prepared *dinner table questions* to stimulate conversation in which all ages could participate:

- What is your favorite toy right now or favorite game to play?
- What book are you reading right now?
- If you could meet anyone from history, who would you meet?
- What does it mean to be a friend?
- What is your favorite holiday?

Another way to stimulate appropriate conversation at the dinner table and go digging for the gold that is in your children's heart is to play the *Hi-Lo* game in which everyone shares their day's high and low moments. This particular game encourages the family to celebrate each other's achievements or blessings. It also stimulates the compassion that is necessary to be empathetic when a family member is hurting. The Hi-Lo game often ended in prayer as our hearts were turned with love and grace to the child who might have been experiencing emotional pain.

Dinnertime was also a time of dreaming together and making future family plans:

- What do you want to do on Saturday? Go to the park? Go swimming?
- Mimi's birthday is coming up. How should we celebrate her?
- Let's make a list of things that we want to do this summer. Then, we can check off the list as we accomplish each one.
- What is the next book we should read together as a family?
- What movie should we watch for movie night this week?
- Is there a friend or a family that you all would like to invite over for dinner on Sunday night? What should we serve? Mexican? Breakfast food?

One of the greatest strengths of a family table comes from the knowledge that no matter what we do, no matter how we fail, we have a place to belong, a place where we will be forgiven, and a place where we will still be loved and welcomed.

—Sally Clarkson

Be Our Guest!

Every Wednesday evening, we invited friends over for a night of food, stimulating conversation, and too much fun to contain. The guests invited to these Wednesday night suppers were single dads and their children, parents and teens, couples dealing with infertility, and anyone else who would like to tag along.

Each Wednesday night had a theme that was announced early in the week so that those coming could prepare.

If *red* was the theme, then every person coming was required to wear something red and bring something red to eat. We would enjoy foods like red gelatin, pizza, spaghetti, tomato salad, and strawberry shortcake.

If *France* was the theme, you must come armed with a tidbit of interesting information about France as well as food that was related to the French culture. We'd have french bread, croissants, chocolate eclairs, salad with french dressing, french onion soup, and french fries.

One of our favorite themes was *good morning!* Each attendee was encouraged to come in their pajamas and bring something that they would eat for breakfast. On these nights, we enjoyed yummy french toast casserole, breakfast tacos, oatmeal with apples, and doughnuts.

 THE POSSIBILITIES ARE ENDLESS FOR THEMES UPON WHICH YOU CAN CREATE AN ENTIRE DINNER PARTY.

The possibilities are endless for themes upon which you can create an entire dinner party. Others that we enjoyed were *the letter S, olé* for a Mexican-themed evening, and *tailgate evening.*

Our family learned the sheer delight of having people in our home and the satisfaction of preparing for and serving others. Because most of these evenings were potluck, it was never too expensive for us as the hosts, but was a much-anticipated break from the weekly routine.

Children need to be taught the virtue of hospitality as soon as they are able to share a toy, snuggle in someone else's lap, and sit at the dinner table with adults. When we open our children's hearts to others through the invitation to be hospitable, they begin to realize that the world doesn't revolve around self but around the joy of serving others.

Be hospitable to one another without complaint. —1 Peter 4:9

Seasonal Traditions

During every season of the year, take at least one family hike along the same route and record the differences that you observe. You can vary this family walk by looking for a specific color or pointing out things that are *God-created* or *man-made* on your journey.

Small children love to collect things on family walks, so give each child a small bag as you leave the house. As he or she collects pretty stones, leaves, acorns, or flowers, you have suddenly acquired the necessary supplies for a lovely centerpiece for the kitchen table.

My favorite type of walk was a quiet walk during which everyone silently observed what was visible. When we arrived at home, it was time to share all of the beauty that we had seen while our tongues were silent but our eyes were active.

Winter

The first snowfall of the winter is a magical day of transformation, a day when the world changes her clothes and becomes a fairyland of ice and snow. Even if you live in a climate where there is no snow and certainly no blizzards, you can still experience winter with exhilaration and energy.

The first day that we observed even a tiny flake outside our living room window was a day that everything else paused and we all trooped into the kitchen to make our favorite chocolate chip cookies. After a brisk walk outside to enjoy the Father's artwork, we would come inside to munch on our cookies and drink a cup of hot chocolate that was bedecked with whipped cream and peppermint candies.

When the snow gathered in abundance outside of our northern home, we often set aside an afternoon to make a snow family that represented each one of us. Some of the children needed Daddy's help and Craig was glad to provide it. It always brought such cheer to our winter hearts to see our family resplendent in scarfs, ball caps, and mittens outside our front windows.

 DURING THE WINTER MONTHS, PLAN SEVERAL FAMILY OR EVEN NEIGHBORHOOD SNOWBALL FIGHTS—WITH A COUPLE OF RULES SO NO ONE GETS HURT.

There was always time during the winter months to plan several family or even neighborhood snowball fights. No one was allowed to deliberately hit someone in the face; the penalty for that was sitting out for a period of time. The snowballs were required to be large and soft—no ice balls for us!—to ensure that no one got hurt. As the years quickly passed and the children grew older, I changed the name of this activity to *the snowball Olympics;* somehow, changing the name took the aggressive nature out of an otherwise fun winter frolic.

When we knew that winter was waning away, we would often make snowballs to put in plastic bags labeled with our names and tuck into the freezer. Then, we looked forward to a day in July when we could retrieve the snowballs from the freezer and take them outside to enjoy.

Whether you experience snow during your winter months or not, you can still use these quiet months to enjoy your family.

The winter months are an ideal time to have a family reading night followed by the extraordinary treat of S'mores over the stove or the fireplace.

On long winter afternoons, I often created a tent using sheets and blankets over the dining room table. The children would bring a book and a stuffed animal into the tent to have a quiet time of reading and snuggling.

Other afternoons, I designed a train using the kitchen and dining room chairs lined up down the hallway. We took turns being the engineer, the caboose, and the passengers. They loved it when I became the steward and served treats to each person on the train.

Winter afternoons and evenings are perfect times to watch classic movies that might otherwise be ignored. Has your family seen *Singin' in the Rain*, *The Absent-Minded Professor*, or the original *Pete's Dragon?*

A sweet winter activity that is sure to bind everyone's hearts together in the warmth of family is watching old family videos or going through the photo books. If you haven't had time to compile your photos into a book, perhaps this winter would be the perfect time to do just that!

Winter is also the perfect time to teach your children the value of writing a letter to a grandparent, a friend who has moved away, or a cousin who lives in another state. Set aside at least one evening during the long months of winter to sit around the family table with popcorn, bright new pens, and stationary. Even the little ones can draw pictures or write their names to send to their Sunday school teacher or the storyteller at the library.

Spring

This season of new birth and joyful expectation is a miraculous opportunity to bask in the wonder of creation as a family. Spring is an invitation from our Creator to be in awe of all that we have been given to steward as caretakers of the world in which we live.

At least once during the months of spring, plan a splash party in the refreshing rain! Go barefoot and allow the water to just pour over your souls that have been frozen by winter. Splash through puddles and find little rivulets of rainwater beside the driveway.

Keep a thermometer outside your kitchen window and record the temperature at the same time every day for a month. Your children will begin to realize that perhaps summer really is on its way as they observe the ever-increasing temperatures.

Spring is the perfect time to plant a family garden and assign each family member a row to take care of as spring gives birth to summer. It is a soul-strengthening activity for each child to be responsible for the growth and eventual flowering or harvesting of a plant.

PLANTING A FAMILY GARDEN IS A SOUL-STRENGTHENING ACTIVITY FOR EACH CHILD.

Springtime is also a sweet opportunity to memorize a Bible verse about the wonder of creation or teach the family a lovely old hymn such as "This Is My Father's World" or "For the Beauty of the Earth."

Ask the Lord *for rain in the springtime; it is the* Lord *who sends the thunderstorms. He gives showers of rain to all people, and plants of the field to everyone.* —Zechariah 10:1 NIV

Summer

The world explodes like a veritable garden of rainbows in the world and mind of a child. Summer is the time for neighborhood kickball games, catching fireflies in the smoky dusk of evening, and feeling the unmatched glee of an ice pop dripping down your chin. Every child needs the long days of summer for exploring, laughing, and lingering. I have heard it said that spring was such a tough act to follow that God decided to create June!

At the onset of summer, invest in a large container of sidewalk chalk. You will never regret it! Our sidewalk and driveway were perpetually decorated by future Rembrandts and Rockwells. Often, an older child hopped on his bike and rode through the neighborhood to collect friends of all ages and sizes. There was nothing more fun than a *sidewalk chalk gallery*. Each participating child drew a picture and then signed his or her name. They were famous in our yard...at least until the next summer rain shower!

A sprinkler, a freezer filled with ice pops, and water balloons are the best gifts that any child can receive on a summer afternoon. Rather than having a classic water balloon fight, our favorite activity was water balloon baseball. This simply requires a bucket or two filled with water balloons, a large yard, and a big plastic bat. The pitcher gently throws a water balloon to the batter and when the bat connected with the water balloon, everyone advanced a base.

EVERY CHILD NEEDS THE LONG DAYS OF SUMMER FOR EXPLORING, LAUGHING, AND LINGERING.

Mornings spent at the park topped off with a picnic with other families spelled *f-u-n* for all of us. The moms were gifted with hours of friendship and much needed adult conversation while the kids became sweaty and tired.

Preschoolers love the endowment of a bucket of water and a paintbrush as they seriously take on the job of *painting* the back deck.

School-age children find extra pleasure in a backyard obstacle course at which they can time each other to see who completes it the fastest.

Jumping rope to the tune of a favorite song can capture the hearts of both girls and boys.

Washing the family cars can be a great activity on a hot summer afternoon followed by cutting open a ripe, luscious watermelon.

You have established all the boundaries of the earth; You have created summer and winter. —Psalm 74:17

As the month of July rolled into August, I was always painfully aware that summer was quickly coming to an end. During the month of August, I scheduled a *Mom date* with each child so that we were able to spend time alone in the midst of a busy family schedule.

Summer only lasts for about ninety-five calendar days each year. After three too-short months of mosquito bites and baseball games, the beach towels will be packed away, the outgrown flip flops will be tossed out, and the lazy, hazy days of summer become a sweaty memory.

The most sobering reality of the sunshiny season of summer is this: you are only given eighteen summers of ninety-five days each to share with your children.

You only have eighteen chances to make dazzling memories, eighteen opportunities to read the books of childhood to your little ones, splash in the sprinkler with them, and make S'mores after a dinner of hot dogs and corn on the cob.

YOU ARE ONLY GIVEN EIGHTEEN SUMMERS OF NINETY-FIVE DAYS EACH TO SHARE WITH YOUR CHILDREN.

You only possess eighteen occasions to spit out watermelon seeds in the front yard, play kick ball all afternoon, and catch fireflies in the summer twilight.

You only are endowed with eighteen shots at teaching your kids to ride their bikes with no hands, play hopscotch on the front sidewalk, and make homemade ice cream before bedtime.

While ninety-five sunshine-filled days seem to fly by, eighteen summers evaporate into adulthood like rain on a hot-tin roof.

In addition to the summer activities that I have already listed, here are just a few more that will last long after autumn has come knocking at your door and well beyond the brevity of eighteen summers.

Make a measuring stick at least six feet tall and about six inches wide. Mark off the inches and the feet on it so it resembles a huge ruler. Hang this piece of wood on a wall in your home and measure your children every year on the first and last days of summer. See how much they have grown during those ninety-five days!

Choose books to read together as a family. Make it a celebration to read the books out loud to your children that were read to you when you were a child. My daughters loved hearing *Tom Sawyer, Mr. Mulligan and His Steam Shovel*, and *Mr. Popper's Penguins* as much as my sons did. And my three sons were as riveted as the girls were by the adventures of *Caddie Woodlawn, The Little House in the Big Woods* series, and *Pippi Longstocking*.

Set aside time every day to read out loud to your children whether they are four years old or fourteen years old. Pop some popcorn, hand out a bowl of fresh strawberries, and put on classical music while you read.

Have you ever thought of sponsoring a contest in your yard once a week? The possibilities are endless! Here are some we enjoyed:

- A watermelon seed spitting contest
- A sidewalk chalk art contest
- A whistling on a piece of grass contest
- A decorate your bike contest
- A who can kick the ball the farthest contest
- A who can hit the baseball the farthest contest
- A squirt-gun contest in the backyard
- A who can say the alphabet backwards contest
- A paper airplane building contest
- A who can memorize the state capitols contest

And then, to add some substance and spiritual growth to your summer, perhaps you could choose a Bible verse for the entire family to memorize each week. Announce the verse of the week every Saturday morning and write it on a white board in your kitchen. Put the weekly verse on the bathroom mirror and on every bedroom door. Then, on Friday afternoon, have each child write out the Bible verse and decorate it with glitter, pieces of fabric, and stickers. Insert each child's page into their own three-ring binder so they have a beautiful, creative record of the Bible verses at the end of the summer.

Summer is a wonderful time to teach your children to embrace the fun and purpose found only in giving to someone else. Volunteer, as a family, to paint a Sunday school room at church. Perhaps you could visit a widow's house and weed her flower beds or wash windows for her. Your children are sure to enjoy making cards and then delivering them to the residents of a local nursing home.

 THE VERY BEST MEMORIES YOU WILL EVER GIVE YOUR CHILDREN ARE FOUND IN THE MEANING OF SERVING OTHERS AND GIVING TO OTHERS.

The very best memories you will ever give your children will not be made at Disney World, at an exotic beach, or even at the neighborhood playground. The very best gift you can give to your children is found in the meaning of serving others and giving to others.

If you can't afford to take a family vacation, make a list of interesting and free places to visit within a two-hour drive from your home. Pack a lunch every Saturday or Sunday and visit these unique places that are within driving distance of where you are raising your family. Make sure that you listen to great music while you drive.

Begin with worship music for the first twenty minutes or so, then listen to Broadway show tunes or Disney songs. Introduce culture with a classical piece or two.

Every family needs a thorough knowledge of and appreciation for patriotic tunes, so sing along to "You're a Grand Old Flag," "Yankee Doodle Dandy," and "God Bless America."

How about playing some popular music from your teenage years? And as always, make sure to end your day with worship.

The youngest members of the family should be encouraged to draw a picture of what they have seen that day. Encourage the school-age children to write a short report on the landmark that you visited.

The ache that fills my heart every year at one minute past September has little to do with the frost on the morning grass or the vibrant colors of the leaves. The ache is birthed in the knowledge that eighteen summers with each child have come and gone. I'll never have the opportunity again to make blueberry ice pops, lay in the grass and name the clouds with a giggling girl, or catch a salamander with a freckle-faced boy.

Ninety-five days. Eighteen summers. That's all you get.

The crickets felt it was their duty to warn everybody that summertime cannot last forever. Even on the most beautiful days in the whole year—the days when summer is changing into fall— the crickets spread the rumor of sadness and change.

—E. B. White, *Charlotte's Web*

Fall

When August packed its bags and left only memories in its wake, I always felt that I was beginning a brand new year on September 1. For some reason, fall heralded the beginning of new dreams, new opportunities, and a new normal. Freshly sharpened pencils, notebooks filled with unmarked pages, and the reality of routine suggested that vacation was over and it was time to enter back into the fray of an organized life.

Life starts all over again when it gets crisp in the fall.
—F. Scott Fitzgerald, *The Great Gatsby*

There is nothing like a fall scavenger hunt to remind us that although we serve a God who never changes, He delights in change! Perhaps your list of items to find could include:

- Pine cone
- Bug
- Puddle
- Cloud
- Cat
- Twig
- Bird
- Evergreen tree
- Red leaf
- Yellow leaf
- Brown leaf
- Pumpkin
- Spider web
- Acorn

After a family walk when everyone gathers these signs of nature, you can then congregate around the kitchen table for a family craft time. After cutting the middle out of a paper plate, glue the leaves around the outside and you have created an autumn wreath.

THERE IS NOTHING LIKE A FALL SCAVENGER HUNT TO REMIND US THAT ALTHOUGH WE SERVE A GOD WHO NEVER CHANGES, HE DELIGHTS IN CHANGE!

Rather than carving pumpkins, our family simply painted them with bright colors and interesting designs.

Autumn is the year's last, loveliest smile.   —William Bryant

Another fall activity was to create paintings with acorns and apples. You can slice an apple through the middle and then dip it into paint and allow your children to make prints on a long piece of paper. The acorns also make interesting shapes when dipped into paint. This can serve as a table runner through the months of September, October, and November.

There are other activities that are ageless and could include grandparents, such as visiting a farm, cider mill, or pumpkin patch, picking apples, or going on a hayride.

One of the highlights of autumn for our family was the bushel of apples that my father always delivered to our front door. We loved discovering different treats that we could make with apples, such as apple oatmeal, baked apples, applesauce, apple cake, and apple crisp. Nothing tastes like fall as much as an apple does!

What fun to have a family game of football in the front yard followed by a bonfire or hotdogs on the grill!

My family always knew that autumn had arrived when I baked my famous pumpkin cookies on a Sunday afternoon while everyone else was watching football. (I share this recipe and others in Appendix B.)

I'm so glad I live in a world where there are Octobers.

—L. M. Montgomery, *Anne of Green Gables*

Every Month of Every Year

January

When the Christmas cards came in the mail throughout the month of December, we used brightly colored yarn to string them in our doorways and across the frosted windowpanes of winter. However, it was during the month of January that these Christmas cards were brought to life around the dinner table. Each evening as the family gathered during the month of January—and often during February and March—one of the children was asked to read a Christmas card out loud to the rest of the family. When we said the blessing for our meal, we also prayed for the family or person who had sent the card to us. It became a lovely way of connecting our children with family members who lived far away as well as our friends from other seasons of life.

January is also a wonderful month to teach your children about the great men and women of other races who have made amazing contributions to the world in which we live. When you are gathered around the dinner table, tell them about Martin Luther King Jr., George Washington Carver, Rosa Parks, Maya Angelou, and Harriet Tubman. Have them read the biographies of Jesse Owens, Frederick Douglass, Booker T. Washington, W. E. B. Du Bois, Michael Jordan, Thurgood Marshall, and Leontyne Price. I hope you and your children have friends of different races and invite them over for dinner often. I believe with my whole heart that it is up to the mothers to teach their children how to love all people of all nations and all socioeconomic levels. If the majority of mothers of this generation would fiercely fight against the racism that is prevalent in society, we would be just one generation from massive and lasting change.

IT IS UP TO THE MOTHERS TO TEACH THEIR CHILDREN HOW TO LOVE ALL PEOPLE OF ALL NATIONS AND ALL SOCIOECONOMIC LEVELS.

February

During the month of February, we listened to the great love songs through the ages. Melodies such as "It Had to Be You," "Always," and "Someone to Watch Over Me" became the soundtrack of our lives during this month set aside for friendship and romance. The highlight of the month of February was the night that we invited both sets of grandparents to our home for dinner by candlelight. The children were required to dress up and use their best manners. The grandparents were thrilled to be invited and tell their grandchildren the details of their love stories and decades-long marriages. At the close of the evening, we prayed for each of our children's future spouses.

Since Presidents' Day occurs in February, spend some time talking about and reading about great American presidents. Teaching your children about George Washington and Abraham Lincoln is a great place to start, but don't forget other presidents like Calvin Coolidge, Dwight D. Eisenhower, and Ronald Reagan. Again, talk about them at the dinner table and read their biographies this month. Teach your children what it means to be an American patriot.

March

The windy month is also known for that great American basketball tradition, March Madness. We are a family whose hearts race with adrenalin at the very mention of this college basketball competition. A family bracket is taped to the refrigerator door so that we can fill in the winners as the tournament takes place. However, the most important aspect of March Madness for the mad McLeod family is that even now, although we are scattered across thousands of miles, each family member fills out their personal family bracket. One family member is appointed to be the scorekeeper and by the end of the month, we have crowned a new McLeod Family March Madness Champion. In years past, when all of the children were at home, the winner was given the opportunity to choose a restaurant for a family celebration. Now, however, the winner receives a gift card to a restaurant for his or her family.

There is one more happy celebration we had this month. Every year, on March 17, I always served green mashed potatoes for dinner in honor of St. Patrick's Day. My children have never forgotten that nonsensical tradition!

April

What fun we have had celebrating April 1 over the years! I always served chicken and green beans for breakfast and a feast of pancakes, bacon, and eggs for dinner. Everyone was expected to bring a brand new joke to the dinner table on April 1.

In our family, everyone received new Easter outfits, compliments of Mimi, my beloved mother. We also had an exciting Easter egg hunt on Easter Sunday afternoon, compliments of Craig's parents, Nanny and Pa. However, the most meaningful part of Easter weekend always occurred on Saturday evening, when Craig read the Easter story out loud to our children. It was important for us to focus on the true meaning of the most important event of the Christian year. We longed for our children to understand the price that had been pain for forgiveness and for eternity.

 THE MONTH OF APRIL IS A PRIME OPPORTUNITY TO EXPOSE YOUR CHILDREN TO OTHER TYPES OF WORSHIP SERVICES.

The month of April is a prime opportunity to expose your children to other types of worship services. We looked for extra services at churches that were different than ours during the season of Lent that culminates in Easter. We attended a Catholic service on the first day of Lent, Ash Wednesday, and a *high church* service on Maundy Thursday. We always tried to include a lively worship service at a historically Black church as well so our children would realize how different Christians express their praise and worship to the Lord.

May

The first day of May has always been so near to my heart. My dear Aunt Marianne Townsend, who also taught me to love reading and later was my high school Latin teacher, introduced me to an unforgettable May tradition when I was just a little girl. Each year on May 1, we delivered bouquets of flowers to the homes of the elderly people in our tiny town. Often, the bouquets were tissue-paper flowers glued lovingly into a construction-paper nosegay. Auntie, as she was adorably known by all of the neighborhood children, taught us to leave the flowers on the porch, ring the doorbell, and then run away. My children participated in this springtime tradition every year until they left home.

The last Monday of the month is the all-American holiday known as Memorial Day and is meant to commemorate men and women who fought bravely to defend our freedoms. On this day, our family paused to listen to the anthems of all of the branches of the military.

June

June 14 is Flag Day, a holiday that is often overlooked. During the month of June, we studied the life of Betsy Ross and Francis Scott Key. I had the little ones color their own flags that they proudly displayed on their bedroom doors or on the kitchen refrigerator. The older children learned the proper way to fold the flag and how to honor and respect it.

Also, during the month of June, we honored the fathers in our lives. The children made their own cards and gifts to give to Craig, their grandfathers, and their uncles. Teaching children how to honor authority figures is a vital part of childhood. I also encouraged the children to make a card or write a letter to another man who had a profound impact on their lives, such as a teacher, a coach, or a neighbor. If you are a single mom, you can still have your children honor those people who have been kind to your family. Honor is not about a holiday, but it is a lifestyle that we must cultivate in our children.

July

 WE MUST MAKE SURE THAT THE NEXT GENERATION UNDERSTANDS THE BLESSINGS AND THE RESPONSIBILITIES OF FREEDOM.

How wonderful it is to live in a free country! We must make sure that the next generation understands the blessings and the responsibilities of freedom. July is the perfect time to talk about the Revolutionary War, the Civil War, World War I, and World War II. Help your children understand the importance of freedom and why it is worth fighting for. If there is a military cemetery in your area, spend some time visiting the graves of the men and women who gave their lives so that we could live in peace.

Fireworks, watermelon, and family yard games were always part of our Fourth of July celebration! Don't let the day pass by without recognizing that freedom is worth celebrating.

> Freedom is never more than one generation away from extinction. We didn't pass it to our children in the bloodstream. It must be fought for, protected, and handed on for them to do the same.
>
> —Ronald Reagan

August

August is the only month in which there are no official holidays. We set aside August as the month that we celebrated our family and our heritage. Declare a random day during the month that belongs especially to your family. Fix a favorite meal, play a family game, and set some goals together. This would be the ideal time to discover the meaning of your surname and everybody's given name. On this personal holiday, which belongs solely to your family, require everyone to come to the dinner table with the same color on to honor your heritage as a team.

August is the perfect month to talk about your family mission statement and write it out on a white board or chalkboard for the entire family to learn and acknowledge. This is the McLeod family mission statement:

> In this family, we honor God with every word we speak and with every action we choose.
> In this family, we love the Bible.
> In this family, we build one another up and we never tear each other down.
> In this family, we share and are generous with our possessions.
> In this family, we cheerfully and willingly serve one another.
> In this family, we are responsible for our own rooms, personal hygiene, and assigned responsibilities.
> In this family, we encourage each other.
> In this family, we choose joy!

September

September marks the end of the glorious days of summer and the beginning of a new school year. On the day before school starts, whether your children attend a public school, a private school, or are homeschooled, have some one-on-one time with each child. Talk about what they are looking forward to and expectations for the year. Listen to their fears or concerns and then pray for each one of them individually. Set priorities for each child when it comes to time management and extracurricular activities. As a parent, you must become the coach as they prepare for a new school year.

If you write out the child's goals at the beginning of the school year, you can then revisit them each semester and on the last day of school.

Be sure to take the requisite photos on the first and last days of school. You will never regret marking and remembering the significance of each year of school.

October

You already know that the day of chief importance in October is the first day of the month, when we begin to play Christmas music in the McLeod home.

This was also the month of taking walks through the crisp leaves and planning an autumn picnic. It was the month of applesauce, apple pie, and apple pancakes. We learned about Johnny Appleseed and the contributions that he made to agriculture.

 WHEREVER YOU LAND ON THE CONTINUUM OF HALLOWEEN, STUDY ITS ORIGINS AND MAKE A PRAYERFUL DECISION.

Halloween is the *stickiest* holiday of the year. Some Christian families observe it, others ignore it, and still others abhor it. Wherever you land on the continuum of Halloween, study its origins and make a prayerful decision. Even if you choose not to observe Halloween, many churches offer alternative events. My mother's philosophy about incorporating Christianity into the challenges of the culture was this, "Whenever you have to say a *no*, be prepared to say a better *yes*." So if you choose not to trick-or-treat, offer a better alternative to your children.

November

For our family, Thanksgiving is a lifestyle, not just a holiday, but we do try to be especially mindful of our blessings during the month of November. When the children were young, I printed out the trunk and branches of a tree for each one of them, along with paper leaf cutouts. Every day, they would write something for which they were thankful on a leaf and it would be added to their tree.

As they grew, we hung a garland across the mantle that was waiting for their leaves of blessing. Every evening at the dinner table, there was a construction leaf by each person's place that they would fill out and explain why they were grateful for a particular blessing; the leaf was then attached to the garland on the mantle.

On the day before Thanksgiving, the entire McLeod family went up a small mountain into the woods in order to select the perfect Christmas tree. Choosing a Christmas tree in the wonder of creation and then cutting it down with your family is a tradition that they will fondly remember.

On Thanksgiving Day, when the children came downstairs, each was given a specific assignment or two in preparation for dinner. The Christmas parades were always on the TV in the background, but everyone was expected to pitch in and help. Some made place cards for the table while others set the table with the fine china and linen napkins. I set bowls on the kitchen counter with a recipe card in each one; whichever bowl you chose was the recipe you were expected to make for Thanksgiving dinner.

When it was time to serve dinner, I always started to cry because I was so grateful for the life that I had been given. Mama's tears are notoriously a part of our Thanksgiving traditions! We then went around the table, from youngest to oldest, to give thanks for our blessings that year.

The day was complete when the pie was put away, the games were brought out, and the family gathered around the piano to sing the carols of Christmas.

We always decorated the Christmas tree on the day after Thanksgiving. After the tree came to life with lights and ornaments in front of our family room windows, we watched *White Christmas*—the best Christmas movie of all time!

December

Oh, my, what a perfectly magical and wondrous month December was in the home of the McLeod family! From the day after Thanksgiving until midnight on New Year's Day, it was a time that was recognized as simply miraculous because of the greatest gift of all: Jesus.

We decorated the family home on the day after Thanksgiving so we were ready to focus on other events and traditions as the month marched toward the most marvelous day in all of history. It was a month of giving, music, and unmatched anticipation.

A HIGHLIGHT OF DECEMBER WAS THE ANNUAL TRIP TO THE DOLLAR STORE, WHEN EACH CHILD TOOK THEIR SAVINGS TO BUY GIFTS FOR FAMILY MEMBERS.

We baked cookies to eat and to give away; we read Christmas stories out loud the entire month of December. A highlight of the month was the annual trip to the dollar store, when each child took their savings to buy gifts for family members—siblings, grandparents, and cousins as well as Mom and Dad. How they loved knowing that they could afford to give to others! *"For God so loved the world, that He gave His only Son"* (John 3:16). We deeply desired for our children to understand that generosity is a secret to an abundant life.

Also, during the month of December, we established the tradition of *secret angels*. On the Sunday afternoon after Thanksgiving, we placed all of the names of the family in a bowl and then each person chose a name. A secret angel might make your bed one morning or unload your portion of the dishwasher. He or she might leave a piece of candy on your pillow at night or an encouraging note on the bathroom mirror. Although the children usually guessed their angel's identity long before the end of the month, the angels would reveal themselves on Christmas Eve morning. Jesus came not to be served but to serve (see Matthew 20:28); we wanted our children to understand that serving others is a key to living like Jesus did.

On Christmas Eve, we all gathered in our favorite place in the entire world: our family room. Little ones sat on their older siblings' laps while Christmas music filled the room. Craig passed around his Bible and each child read a portion of the Christmas story out loud. Even the youngest, who was unable to read, said her verses out loud that her older brother whispered into her ear. The tears always began to flow down my cheeks as I gazed into the eyes and into the hearts of the most precious gifts I had ever been given—my children. After the astounding yet personal account of the Christmas story had been read, we gathered to pray and then to sing the songs of Christmas around the piano. Then, it came time for each one to hang their stockings on the mantle, from the oldest to the youngest.

 ON NEW YEAR'S EVE, WE ASKED EACH CHILD FOR A HIGHLIGHT FROM THE PAST YEAR AND A GOAL FOR THE COMING YEAR.

During the week between Christmas and New Year's Eve, Craig and I prayed and asked God to give us a Scripture for each child for the coming year. We recorded these Scriptures in the family notebook and then gave the Scriptures to our children on New Year's Eve. We also took the time to pray the verse over our child's life while we were gathered together. Also on New Year's Eve, we asked each child for a highlight from the past year and a goal for the coming year. Those were also recorded in the family notebook. What a joy it is now to look back over the years and read the goals, the highlights, and the Scripture verses!

Throughout the year, I saved the extra napkins from the various holidays and events and placed them together in a plastic bag in the pantry. In my napkin collection, I might have napkins from my parents' anniversary celebration and basketball napkins from a son's birthday party. There would likely be Valentine's Day napkins, Fourth of July napkins, and ballet napkins from a little girl's party. We used these napkins for our New Year's Eve celebration so that we could remember the celebrations of the year that had just passed.

In the end, I am the only one who can give my children a happy mother who loves life. —Janene Wolsey Baadsgaard

It Only Takes Time

I hope that you have enjoyed reading this chapter as much as I have loved walking through the memories of all that happened in the family room and the McLeod home. This chapter tells the story of the events, the traditions, the love, and the fun that crafted the heart of our family. You, too, will tell the story of your family someday, so make it a good one!

The only thing that you really need to decorate the family room of your heart is time. This room is not decorated with expensive trips, designer clothes, or $1,000 birthday parties; it's adorned by you and your presence. You must spend time in the family room of your heart, my friend, in order to create a lasting legacy that your children will take into the families that they create someday.

 YOU MUST SPEND TIME IN THE FAMILY ROOM OF YOUR HEART IN ORDER TO CREATE A LASTING LEGACY THAT YOUR CHILDREN WILL TAKE INTO THE FAMILIES THAT THEY CREATE SOMEDAY.

Precious mother, I know that you are overwhelmed with the everydayness of life and you might feel that your children have a never-ending capacity to rely solely on you. You might falsely yet sincerely believe that your world is a small place and that no one sees you.

To the world you may be one person but to one person you may be the world. —Taylor Hanson

Your heart is the center of your children's solar system and you must remind yourself that their little lives revolve around you. You are their happiness, their constant, their warmth, and their sunshine. You are their home, their song, their hope, and their source. I hope that even when the sink is filled with dishes, when the laundry basket is overflowing, and when you haven't washed your hair in days, you will know how irreplaceable you are in the family room.

Traditions are the stories that families write together. The stories that tradition writes are found on the hearts of your children long after they are grown and gone. Keep writing your story, dear mom.

The greatest legacy we can leave our children is happy memories.
—Og Mandino

12

The Kitchen

Taste and see that the Lord is good; how blessed is the man who
takes refuge in Him!   —Psalm 34:8

Mmmm...do you smell that delicious aroma? Can you even imagine
what will be served in the kitchen of your heart?

If the mother is the heart of the family, then the kitchen is the heart of the
home. The kitchen is the place where scrumptious meals are prepared, where
love is tasted, and where genuine care for one another is a delicious aroma. A
kitchen is often the room in the family home where games are played, where
conversations are rich, and where understanding is served generously.

Even now, when my husband and I sit at our oak table by ourselves, I can
still hear the laughter of yesterday and smell the joy of sharing a meal with
those precious little ones given to Craig and me.

The savory meals that are served in the kitchen take forethought and
work, but a mother completes these tasks out of love. I knew, when I was in the
trenches of motherhood, that I could serve chicken tenders and french fries
out of bags from the frozen aisles at the supermarket, but it wouldn't create

the same memories or present the same love as did a meal of baked chicken, smashed potatoes, green beans, and a homemade strawberry pie. As a mother, I wanted to present meals that were not only delectable but also filled with nutrients and vitamins. It was no easy task to feed a family of seven night after night but I knew that it was one of the most tangible ways in which I, as the mother, demonstrated my perpetual and enthusiastic love.

 IT'S NO EASY TASK TO FEED A FAMILY NIGHT AFTER NIGHT BUT IT'S ONE OF THE MOST TANGIBLE WAYS TO DEMONSTRATE YOUR PERPETUAL AND ENTHUSIASTIC LOVE.

When I prepared meals, I was also preparing the atmosphere, the conversation, and the memories.

In the kitchen of your heart, you are also preparing a feast of emotional and spiritual vitamins for your children. If you are not looking well to the ways of your heart, you will be unable to look well to the ways of your household. It is in the kitchen of a mother's heart where healthy emotions and spiritual habits are prepared to nourish the health of her family.

It is no secret that motherhood can be exhausting; there are many days when you feel that you are scraping the bottom of your emotional barrel. But may I share a secret with you in the kitchen of your heart? I do believe that it is in the plan of God for the years of mothering to be emotionally abundant years for a woman, not years of emotional famine. God desires for the season of constant mothering to be years of satisfying memories and refreshing strength for you; this is why we will spend some time in the kitchen of your heart.

Kitchen: Noun: A gathering place for friends and family; a place where memories are made and seasoned with love.

—Emma Reed

Supermom Doesn't Live in the Kitchen

You don't have to pretend to be *supermom* because you have a super God who is available to you at any time of the day or night. It is in the kitchen of your heart that His presence is the most appetizing and His characteristic flavor is at its most intense. This is the place where you marinate in all that He is and in all that He has for you.

As a mother, you must set aside time to spend with the Lord every day during these years. Even if it is only five minutes, you will be surprised at the way that it stabilizes your emotions and creates a loving atmosphere in your home. Even if all you do is read one verse of Scripture in the morning, it will still flavor your life with the sweet goodness of the Lord.

Sometimes, if you are in the season of babies and toddlers, *quiet times* are actually not very quiet! Often during those years, I would read my Bible out loud to a nursing baby or a fussy toddler. Just the cadence of my voice brought a fragrance into our world that was comforting and peaceful. During the years of lively preschoolers, I would allow them to watch a Christian video while I read my Bible with a cup of coffee. What fun!

As the children grew, I found that worshipping with my children was one of my favorite activities of the day. We played worship music, sang, and danced together in the safety of our home. Often, one of the older children read out loud from an age-appropriate devotional and then we discussed it as a family. While my children were being nourished spiritually, I was also growing in my faith.

THERE WILL BE SO MANY TIMES YOU FEEL LIKE YOU'VE FAILED, BUT IN THE EYES, HEART, AND MIND OF YOUR CHILD, YOU ARE SUPERMOM!

There will be so many times you feel like you've failed, but in the eyes, heart, and mind of your child, you are supermom!

It's in the kitchen of your heart where you must set your priorities. If you are not healthy spiritually, then you will never be healthy emotionally. You will never be the stable emotional mother that you desire to be for your children until you put first things first. You must serve yourself a heaping portion of intimacy with Christ every day in order for you to prepare the appropriate emotions to serve your children.

When my home was overrun with children, toys, dogs, books, balls, and a demanding schedule, I traded children with a friend for one morning each month. I took her children one morning and she would take mine the next morning. The trade enabled each of us to have our own personal retreat and refill our empty hearts with the stability of Christ.

Do you not know? Have you not heard? The Everlasting God, the Lord, *the Creator of the ends of the earth does not become weary or tired. His understanding is unsearchable. He gives strength to the weary, and to the one who lacks might He increases power. Though youths grow weary and tired, and vigorous young men stumble badly, yet those who wait for the* Lord *will gain new strength; they will mount up with wings like eagles, they will run and not get tired, they will walk and not become weary.*   —Isaiah 40:28–31

Guard Your Heart and Your Tongue

With an age difference of nearly fourteen years between my first child and my last, I was dealing with driver's permits and dirty diapers, or potty training and preparing for the prom, all during the same season.

When my children were toddlers, I could probably have been classified as an overprotective mother. I made sure that my sweet babies would never be able to tamper with the cleaning supplies that were under the kitchen sink. I had child locks on all of my cabinets until they all had gone away to college!

One evening, after a very long day of homeschooling, teaching Latin, folding laundry, and dealing with the liveliness that belonged solely to Jordan, our third son, I was spent both emotionally and spiritually. One of the teenagers was being very persistent in a request that I had earlier refused; the conversation went on longer than was healthy for either of us. I finally erupted and spewed harsh, unkind words on this hormone-laced young man. He stomped off to bed and I cried myself to sleep.

The next morning, when I was having my treasured quiet time, I read the following verse:

Death and life are in the power of the tongue, and those who love it will eat its fruit. —Proverbs 18:21

I heard the endearing voice of the Holy Spirit say to me, "Carol, you need to lock up your tongue just like you have locked up the poison cleaning products under your sink. Your tongue is not bringing life to your teenagers. You need to guard your heart and your tongue."

YOU NEED TO LOCK UP YOUR TONGUE JUST LIKE YOU HAVE LOCKED UP THE POISON CLEANING PRODUCTS UNDER YOUR SINK.

One of the primary ways in which we mother the flock of little people who are gathered around our knees is by our emotions and our tongues. When our tongue is out of control, it is a heart issue. As a mother, I reminded myself often that my emotions did not control me, but that I controlled my emotions. There were many moments in my mothering journey when anger and frustration threatened to bubble up and spill out. In those moments, I would turn the heat down by making the decision to sing and pray. I discovered that quoting the Word, breaking out into song, and choosing to pray rather than to pounce on one of my children actually enabled me to view those temporary circumstances with the eyes of eternity.

The heart of the righteous ponders how to answer, but the mouth of the wicked pours out evil things. —Proverbs 15:28

One method of self-control that aided me greatly was to simply make a list of the things that I was allowed to say on a daily basis:

+ I love you and I like you!

+ You are such a good boy!

+ You are smart and you are a good obeyer!

+ You are important to me. I am so thankful to be your mom.

As I rehearsed and memorized the list of acceptable statements, it changed my heart from frustrated to fulfilled. I realized that I needed to think and pray before I spoke rather than simply *feel* before I spoke.

> The heart of the wise instructs his mouth and adds persuasiveness to his lips.
> —Proverbs 16:23

I also crafted a very strict list of phrases and sentences that I was *never* allowed to speak over my children:

- I don't like you very much right now.

- You are driving me crazy.

- Why won't you obey me? You are a difficult child.

- I wish that you lived somewhere else.

- Why can't you be more like…

- I love you but I just don't like you very much.

I had allowed my tongue to be led by my emotions to such a great degree that it was paramount for me to be very assertive about taking back the control of it. Every morning, while I was brushing my teeth, I declared out loud, "This mouth will only be used today to encourage and instruct my children. It is not a tongue of anger, frustration, or cruel tones."

 WHEN CHILDREN REQUIRE CORRECTION OR INSTRUCTION, AS ALL CHILDREN DO, ENDEAVOR TO ACCOMPLISH IT WITH A SPIRIT OF LOVE AND KINDNESS.

When my children required correction or instruction, as all children do, I would endeavor to accomplish it with a spirit of love and kindness. I only allowed myself to yell or raise my voice when one of my children was in immediate danger.

I was a firm mother and was definitely in charge of my five strong-willed children. I made sure they knew that I was the boss; they probably thought I was overly strict at times. However, I was determined never to be cruel, heartless, or overly emotional in my dealings with them.

The mother is the heart of the home and she must lead by example. Your home will only be as happy as you are, as peaceful as you are, as kind as you are, and as joyful as you are. If you are easily frustrated with your children, then they will become easily frustrated with one another.

> We need to think of our tongue as a messenger that runs errands for our heart. Our words reveal our character.
>
> —Chuck Swindoll

Give Yourself a Break!

Craig and I lived in a very small home when we brought our fifth baby home from the hospital. Financially, we were unable to move into a bigger home, so there were often toys scattered across the family room floor, unfolded laundry on the couch, and breakfast dishes still on the table.

On one such morning when I was nursing the baby in the living room while the other children were playing or completing school assignments, my mom stopped by to check on me. It was always a delight to have her presence in my home. She was a very successful realtor and was inevitably dressed impeccably, looking like she had stepped off the cover of *Vogue* magazine and was on her way to lunch at the country club.

I looked at my beautiful mom and then down at myself. I wasn't wearing any makeup; in fact, I hadn't even brushed my hair yet. I was wearing sweatpants and one of Craig's oversized T-shirts because of the recent pregnancy. There was baby spit-up on my shoulder and a toddler clamoring to sit on my lap. In that instant, post-pregnancy hormones took over and I started to cry.

"Oh, Mom," I told her tearfully, "I am so sorry that my house looks like this. I am so sorry that you have to walk in and see the mess and smell the smells and observe the chaos."

"Honey," she lovingly replied, "what you are doing today is so much more important than what I am doing. I think that you are doing great! This is exactly how a house with five wonderful children is supposed to look!"

And then with grace and compassion, she held the toddler while tackling the mountain of laundry on my couch. I have never forgotten her words and I have repeated them often over the years to other young moms.

Emotionally healthy moms know that raising their children is more impactful and significant than what happens in the White House on any given day. What you are investing in your family's lives holds greater eternal significance than the gains and losses of Wall Street.

WHAT YOU ARE INVESTING IN YOUR FAMILY'S LIVES HOLDS ETERNAL SIGNIFICANCE.

You don't need to plan Pinterest quality birthday events to be a wonderful mom.

Your home does not need to be immaculate twenty-four hours a day to be impressive.

You don't need to put on makeup every morning by 6:30 a.m. to be beautiful.

You don't need to cook gourmet meals in order to feed your family.

Your home doesn't need to have the visual appearance of one that has been decorated by Joanna Gaines.

The atmosphere of your home is more telling than its décor. The menu of your heart is more meaningful than what is on the menu for dinner.

These years will never come again, dear mother. Believe me, I know. You have only two priorities during these wonderful, busy years—Jesus and your family.

Now, I am not giving you permission to live in a mountain of garbage nor am I applauding you for ordering pizza every night for dinner. An orderly home will definitely deliver more peace to your family life than will a pigpen. However, a mound of laundry on the couch, Legos in the middle of the family room floor, and toothpaste on the bathroom mirror are all part of the happy disarray that accompanies these years.

The messy beauty of motherhood may be the season of life that you are currently living in. When fall arrives, there are certainly leaves on the ground; when it's winter's turn, there is snow everywhere. If you are in the season of the *little years*, it should be no surprise that there are always dishes to be done, beds to be made, and crayon markings to scrub off the walls.

Mom, I want to remind you today that you matter. Every word that you speak, every book that you read, and every song that you sing matters to the astonishing plan of God in your life. So give yourself a break and enjoy these years with no expectation of perfection.

> Successful mothers are not the ones who have never struggled but they are the ones that never give up despite the struggles.
> —Sharon Jaynes

A Tribe

You need a tribe of women who will stand with you and stay with you during these sometimes frustrating but always fulfilling years of life. In other cultures and at other times in history, women gathered at quilting bees or at church dinners. They circled the wagons around a campfire and exchanged wisdom and advice; barn raisings were an opportunity for families to help one another and for women to have much needed companionship. My grandmother, mother, and aunts used to sit on the front porch and snap green beans or shell peas while they talked about recipes, soothing the babies, and their limited budgets.

In the twenty-first century, we have a tendency to live in isolation. Social media may sometimes feel like a community, but it's really just technology. If all you are doing, as a mother, is looking at other moms' Instagram accounts, then you are missing the heart of healthy relationships.

IF ALL YOU ARE DOING IS LOOKING AT OTHER MOMS' INSTAGRAM ACCOUNTS, THEN YOU ARE MISSING THE HEART OF HEALTHY RELATIONSHIPS.

This has always been a challenge for me because I am an introvert. To be honest, I am happier with a book and a cup of coffee than I am spending time with a lot of people. However, my husband—who has never met a stranger, only friends he doesn't yet know—has convinced me that life is bigger than the chair in front of my fireplace. He has encouraged me over the years that we, as God's children, are wired for relationships and for friendship.

Not abandoning our own meeting together, as is the habit of some people, but encouraging one another. —Hebrews 10:25

We need each other, moms. The Father didn't design us to be *Lone Ranger* Christians or lonely mothers. We were not created to live on the island of social isolation. You, as a mother, are in a season of life where you desperately need the safety and encouragement of dear friends. And, if you would graciously allow me to get back on my soapbox for just another minute, make sure that your tribe includes a couple of older moms as well as your peers.

Similarly, teach the older women to live in a way that honors God. They must not slander others or be heavy drinkers. Instead, they should teach others what is good. These older women must train the younger women to love their husbands and their children, to live wisely and be pure, to work in their homes, to do good, and to be submissive to their husbands. Then they will not bring shame on the word of God. —Titus 2:3–5 NLT

The Bible says it is vital for young women to allow older women to have a role in their lives. It is actually a comfort to listen to the voice of experience when it comes to building a vibrant and solid marriage, loving your children with creativity and patience, and establishing a peaceful and joyful home. The best part about having a mentor mom in your life is that you can ask her questions that perhaps no one else can answer for you:

- How old were your children when you potty trained them? If you had to do it again, when would you begin to potty train? Do you have any tips for me?

- What recipes did your family really enjoy? How did you feed five children on such a strict budget?

- What were your family traditions that your children still talk about?

- What did you do when your child had a temper tantrum? How did you handle temper tantrums in public?

- Please give me some advice about parenting teenagers. I feel like they don't love me anymore. How can that be?

- Was your husband an involved father?

- How can I keep the romance alive in my marriage when I am so tired at night?

The stability and strength that an older mom will bring into your life will impact your family for generations.

Create a safe environment with your tribe of moms where you can share strengths and weaknesses and pray for one another. You need women in your life who will encourage you on your motherhood journey and moms whom you can encourage as well.

One of my favorite places of friendship happened when I planned play dates for my children at a local park. While the children played ball or busied their little bodies on the playground, the mothers gathered in chairs or at a picnic table and then talked the afternoon away. It was a healthy time for me to hear their hearts and share my needs with them.

Often, we would invite a family over for dinner. While the fathers played with the children in the yard, they encouraged the moms to go for a walk together. Even doing the dishes with another woman is more fun than doing them alone!

 EVEN DOING THE DISHES WITH ANOTHER WOMAN IS MORE FUN THAN DOING THEM ALONE!

As a pastor's wife, I often planned *girls' night out* events for the women at church. Sometimes we would simply gather at the church for desserts, Bible study, and conversation. Other times, we might meet at an inexpensive restaurant or at someone's home for a shared meal.

The answer to your loneliness is in your hands, dear mom. This is one area of life where you must be assertive and reach out to other women who might need you more than you need them.

In him you too are being built together to become a dwelling in which God lives by his Spirit. —Ephesians 2:22 NIV

Leave the Past in the Past

If you truly desire to serve a delicious childhood and a scrumptious family life to your children with a garnish of joy, then you will learn to leave the past in the past.

If you grew up in an angry, volatile home, leave the past in the past.

If you lost your temper just yesterday with your children, leave the past in the past.

If you and your husband had a whopper of a disagreement last night, leave the past in the past.

If you have regrets about your young adulthood, leave the past in the past.

You will discover that if you sincerely thirst to be a healthy mom who serves a consistently nutritious home experience to her family, then you will not allow past mistakes to torment you today.

Brothers and sisters, I do not regard myself as having taken hold of it yet; but one thing I do: forgetting what lies behind and reaching forward to what lies ahead, I press on toward the goal for the prize of the upward call of God in Christ Jesus. —Philippians 3:13–14

If you exhibited the bitter fruit of impatience to your children, apologize quickly and then dish up an afternoon of sweet peace and joy. If you were spicy or harsh with your baby during the middle of the night, apologize even to your baby and then spend time just cuddling and speaking sweet words of assurance over this little life.

If you have a history of being an angry and unsettled mom, leave that mom in the past. Don't bring her into today. Be the mom that your kids need today; refuse to be haunted by the ghosts of your childhood or by the mistakes that you made yesterday.

Do not call to mind the former things, or consider things of the past. Behold, I am going to do something new, now it will spring up; will you not be aware of it? I will even make a roadway in the wilderness, rivers in the desert. —Isaiah 43:18–19

Today is a new day to be the mom that you have always wanted to be! Be that mom today!

One of the main reasons that every mom needs to leave the past in the past is so that she is able to enjoy the glory that is today. A mother who is living in today, not in yesterday or tomorrow, is able to fully appreciate the little arms that are wrapped around her neck and the sweet sounds of her own children's voices. When your heart is firmly planted in the fertile soil of today, you will relish the call to motherhood as never before.

Mom, you are the only one who can serve up eighteen years of healthy and nutritious memories to your children. You are the only one who is able to ensure that your children experience a happy today. You simply must be fully invested in the sumptuous flavor of today. Give yourself fully to the task before you: raising children who are secure in their family home, cheerfully submitted to their mother's authority, and lovingly embraced in her heart.

A mother must set her mind, her emotions, and her heart on present-tense living. She must determine to be fully *there* in every moment with her children. When you are up to your elbows in the stew of giggles, loose teeth, and science projects, you are at your very best. This type of living is so much more satisfying than an immaculate home, perfectly applied makeup, or a designer wardrobe. It's a delicious life!

In the childhood memories of every good cook, there's a large kitchen, a warm stove, a simmering pot and a mom.
—Barbara Costikyan

13

The Laundry Room

Create in me a clean heart, God, and renew a steadfast spirit within me. —Psalm 51:10

It was a Sunday morning and, as usual, we were running late for church. I needed to find a clean pair of socks for a half-dressed child but I was facing a small but obstructing dilemma. I couldn't even open the laundry room door because the dirty laundry was piled so high against it. It was impossible to reach the clean clothes in the dryer because the soiled ones had exploded all over the laundry room.

Frustrated, I began to push against the laundry room door with all my might until I could just reach my arm in far enough to open the dryer door. One by one, through a tiny crack, I removed pieces of laundry from the dryer until I finally felt the orphaned sock. By this time, I was sweating profusely and we were even later for church than before. As I closed the door so I was no longer held captive by the grimy, messy pile of clothing and towels in the small laundry room, I heard the Holy Spirit whisper to me, "Carol, the laundry is like the poor: you will always have it with you!"

Did you know that the Holy Spirit has a sense of humor? How wonderful to be able to giggle with the Holy Spirit at the perpetual parade of stained clothes that kept me busy day after day!

The teenage years usher in a new season of training and oversight. Yesterday's lessons will be forgotten in the wake of hormones, acne, driving permits, college entrance exams, and first love. It is during these tempestuous yet treasured years that you will need to develop a stronger relationship with this newly budding adult that will withstand the threat of the culture and the testing of desired independence. Even when it is difficult or embarrassing, you must deal with the laundry piling up in your teen's heart. You must talk about personal hygiene, money issues, appropriate manners, and nutritious eating. You may feel as if you are sorting out life one load at a time.

EVEN WHEN IT IS DIFFICULT OR EMBARRASSING, YOU MUST DEAL WITH THE LAUNDRY PILING UP IN YOUR TEEN'S HEART.

So many issues in life threaten to leave a residue of frustration and filth that clouds the endurance of a family's capacity to thrive. The teenage years can be messy, sullied, and even nasty if the mother doesn't realize the importance of being diligent in the laundry room of her heart. The laundry room is comparable to the years of dealing with teenage issues and temperaments. If you, dear mom, determine to be diligent in the laundry room, you will discover that the teenage years can be loads of fun!

If you are not diligent while your child is between the ages of thirteen and twenty, you might lose control over the contamination that the culture brings into your home and the teenage hormones that threaten to take over what was formerly an orderly family life. It takes sorting through issues with your teen, being quick to spot any stains, and removing them immediately. Finally, it requires attention to the wrinkles in life. Let's get to it!

I know what it's like to finish the laundry and to look in the basket five minutes later and it's full again.   —Ann Romney

Teens vs. Toddlers

When I was a young mom and desperate for any type of wisdom that an older mom could give me, I had the luxury of staying in the home of a woman who had mentored me for nearly ten years. I brought my two preschool boys with me for a week of encouragement, strength, and insight. At the time, Carolyn had two children in high school. I noticed how diligent she was to go into her children's bedrooms every night and spend time sitting on their beds while they debriefed with their mom about their day.

When I mentioned this sweet ritual to Carolyn after I had been there just a few days, she looked into my tired eyes and quietly said, "Carol, if you do it right, teenagers take much more time than toddlers do."

At the time, I couldn't imagine anything that took more time than the constant oversight and demands that came with being the mom of two lively, inquisitive preschool boys. Through the years, however, I remembered her words as well as her example. When the teenage years quickly arrived, I was prepared and knew that one of the most important gifts that I could offer to my children was time.

 THE MOTHER OF A TEENAGER MUST BE WILLING TO LISTEN WHEN THEY ARE READY TO TALK—EVEN AT 3 A.M.

The mother of a teenage son or daughter must be willing to listen when they are ready to talk. If your child comes into your room at 3 a.m. and says, "Mom, I need to talk to you," you must throw off the covers, wipe the sleep from your eyes, and be ready to listen with your whole heart. If your teenager comes into the family room just when you are ready to relax with a good book and says, "Mom, I need to talk to you," you must cheerfully put the book aside and give them your full attention.

Some of the happiest times of my brood's teenage years happened in the evening when I would venture into their messy rooms with books, uniforms, and shoes scattered all around; I would just sit on their bed and listen amid the mountain of mess. If they didn't want to talk, I began to ask probing questions:

- What did you have for lunch today?

- Who did you sit with at lunch?

- Who is your favorite teacher?

- Do you have a lot of homework tonight?

- What made you happy today?

- Is there anything that you want to tell me?

Sorting through the issues of life with your teen will require masses of your time but it will be more than worth it. When you exchange your valuable time for the opportunity to build a bridge of communication with your teen, you will be developing a friendship for life.

 WHEN YOU TAKE THE OPPORTUNITY TO BUILD A BRIDGE OF COMMUNICATION WITH YOUR TEEN, YOU WILL BE DEVELOPING A FRIENDSHIP FOR LIFE.

I told my children during these years that they could talk to me about anything that they wanted to talk about and say anything that they wanted to say. However, there were some guidelines for this type of communication; they were required to speak respectfully with a proper tone of voice, use kind verbiage, and not scowl, smirk, or display any other sour expression on their face. If they failed to do so, I would say something like, "Can you please say that in a nicer way?" Often they had to repeat a sentence and change their inflection or their choice of words, but it encouraged proper communication during the heated hours of life.

My daughter Joy, who has always lived up to her name, has told me that one of the things that she remembers about her teenage years is that I would often quietly whisper to her, "Fix your face." She knew that it was time to wipe the sullen look off and replace it with a pleasant expression.

The Grand Inquisition

I not only dogged my teenage progeny with never-ending questions, but I also interviewed their friends relentlessly. It didn't matter if a friend had been in my home every day of the year or if this was his or her first visit; I viewed it as my personal responsibility to get to know this person well and quickly. I would ask the newcomers:

+ What does your father do? Does your mom work outside the home?

+ Do you have siblings? How many? Do you like your siblings?

+ Where do you go to church? What did the pastor talk about last week?

+ What is your favorite thing to do outside of school?

+ What kind of music do you listen to? What is your favorite movie?

I rather believe that the young adults who were brave enough to cross the threshold of our home enjoyed the attention and the interview.

When our son Christopher was a sophomore in high school, he took world history from everyone's favorite teacher, Mrs. Buffalo. As she was preparing this class of future leaders for the midterm exam, she asked, "What was the Grand Inquisition?"

Michael Talley, who was a pastor's son and now pastors a growing church, raised his hand frantically, so Mrs. Buffalo called on him.

"The Grand Inquisition is what happens when you go to Mrs. McLeod's house," he quipped.

He was right—and I am proud of it!

One of the greatest delights in life is embracing the influence you can have on the life of a teenager—whether it is your own or one of their peers. Invite your sons' and daughters' friends over for a night of pizza, games, and conversation. If money is a challenge, have everyone chip in a couple of dollars. Listen to their conversations and carefully insert your opinion when possible.

THE HOURS THAT MY TEENAGERS' FRIENDS SPENT AROUND MY KITCHEN TABLE ARE AMONG THE HAPPIEST HOURS OF MY LIFE.

My home was never the finest and my cuisine was never expensive but the hours that my teenagers' friends spent around my kitchen table are among the happiest hours of my life. We had an *open door* policy at the McLeod home; anyone was welcome at any time. I will admit that there were days when I didn't know how I would stretch a meal or when my soul ached for time alone, but I was willing to invest in the lives of the opinionated, loud, and energetic folks who showed up at my door during those years.

Love Language

It has always been so amazing to me that children raised in the same home—with the same parents, same socioeconomic level, and same basis of faith—can turn out so differently! It was during those insightful teenage years that I realized just how different all of my children were.

I am a hugger and a toucher by nature. When our first son Matthew was about fourteen years old, I was shocked that he recoiled every time that I reached out to touch him. I wondered, *What happened to the child who loved to sit on my lap and snuggle with his mom?* The larger question was, *How can I continue to show my love for my firstborn son without driving him away?*

A dear friend recommended that I read *The 5 Love Languages* by Gary Chapman[7] in my quest to express love to this newly birthed teenage boy. I realized that Matt's love language was gifts, not physical touch. I had to change my strategy for revealing my great love for this firstborn son of my heart. So rather than hug or kiss him on his way out the door in the morning, I'd say, "Matt, there is an extra dollar on the counter for you to buy a Gatorade after practice." My boy instantly turned into that precious little person who loved his mother's attention as he picked up the dollar and gave me a quick kiss on the cheek before he left.

When Christopher, our second son, traveled through his teenage years, he didn't require money or gifts; he merely wanted my words of encouragement. I remember one afternoon when he walked forlornly into the kitchen, discouraged by a teacher and overwhelmed by academics. I looked into his blue eyes, which had lost their sweet sparkle, and said sincerely, "Chris, I think that you are doing great! You are kind to your family and Dad so appreciates you serving on the worship team at church. I am so pleased with you."

---

7. Gary Chapman, *The 5 Love Languages: The Secret to Love That Lasts* (Chicago: Northfield Publishing, 1992).

He looked at me with just a little more life in his eyes and said, "Really, Mom? Really? You think I'm doing good?"

I continued to give him words of encouragement as he dealt with the ups and downs of teenage life in America.

And then there was Jordan. I was thrilled to realize that Jordan's love language was touch. He would slide up close to me while I was doing the dishes or folding laundry, put his arm around me in church, and hold my hand at the mall.

One of the delights of the years of parenting healthy, productive teenagers is to discover the manner in which they receive love. Each one of our growing children is developing differently and has been wired by their Creator to accept affection in a unique manner. You, as the mom, hold the key to discovering each one's preference.

Everything

When I was a young mom with just two small boys, I loved to ask older moms for advice. I kept a small journal of all the words of wisdom that motherhood sages offered as I interviewed each one intently.

After Craig and I moved to North Carolina to pastor a church when Matt was six and Chris was four, I was thrilled to have a whole new crop of experienced moms to interrogate. One of the women whose wisdom literally dripped out of her pores was Mrs. Brisson, affectionately known as "Mrs. B" by the church members and "Ga-Ga" by all of her young Sunday school students. Mrs. B not only taught Sunday school but she also played the piano, kept the church books, and planned all of the women's events. This wizened, white-haired little woman was a force to be reckoned with!

As the new pastor's wife, I was invited to her home one afternoon for iced tea and her famous cookies. I couldn't wait to interview her...and apparently, she couldn't wait to interview me either. However, when I convinced her to talk about motherhood, her planned examination of me was aborted; she joyfully and fully offered advice for all seasons of motherhood.

Mrs. B gave me one particular piece of prudence that remained in my heart for many years and truly guided my decisions a decade later as the mother of teenagers. She told me, "Carol, when your children are teenagers, let them go to every Christian event that they ask to attend. Let them go to youth group, camp, Christian concerts, and even youth group at other churches. Even if their motive is wrong for wanting to go to a certain event, the Holy Spirit will be there speaking to your child."

WHEN YOUR CHILDREN ARE TEENS, LET THEM GO TO EVERY CHRISTIAN EVENT THAT THEY ASK TO ATTEND. EVEN IF THEIR MOTIVES ARE WRONG, THE HOLY SPIRIT WILL BE SPEAKING TO YOUR CHILD.

Mrs. B continued her train of thought with this final admonition, "Don't ever punish your child by disallowing them to go to youth group, church, or a Christian event. When your child is struggling with their behavior issues, that's exactly where they need to be!"

Her words echoed often through my soul during the nearly twenty-year span when one of my children was a teenager. Although sometimes it was a sacrifice, every time one of our offspring asked to attend a Christian event, the answer was always, "Sure, we can make that work." If a family function had been planned first, then we would see if there was something else that the child could do at another time. Christian camp, concerts, Bible studies, youth groups, ski trips, retreats, and Christian festivals were all an automatic *yes* in our home.

If a teenager had not obeyed and had chosen to do something that was unacceptable, the punishment never involved abstaining from a Christian event. The teen was disciplined but not denied the opportunity to grow in his or her faith.

When you are in the throes of parenting a teenager, it might seem easier to refuse him or her the opportunity to do something that's generally fun like a Christian youth event—but don't do it. As I observe my years of parenting teens through the rearview mirror of life, I am grateful for every connection that my child had with the body of Christ. Often when one of my teens returned home from summer camp, a mission trip, or even a simple church gathering, his or her heart was softer and more sensitive to the ways of the Lord because they had been in communion with the Holy Spirit.

To this day, I believe that Mrs. B got it right!

Show Up!

Life can be so busy at times and as the mother of the family, you might feel as if you are being pulled in hundreds of different directions. The years of parenting teenagers are among the busiest years of your life. Some days, you might feel as if you meet yourself coming and going out the front door!

YOU WILL NEVER REGRET SHOWING UP FOR THE EVENTS IN WHICH YOUR TEENS ARE INVOLVED AND BEING A VISIBLE PART OF THEIR EXTRACURRICULAR LIFE.

Although this season requires hustling, scheduling, and even juggling, you will never regret showing up for the events in which your teens are involved and being a visible part of their extracurricular life. If there is a ball game, be there. If your teen is in a concert, forfeit your exercise routine and be there. If there is a recital, reschedule your Bible study and go to the recital. If there is a class play, spelling bee, or science fair, it is not only the most important thing in your teen's life but it should be the most important thing in your life as well. Whatever your teenager is involved in, whether it is a major event or a minor one, you need to be in attendance cheering wildly.

Gifts do not replace the importance of just showing up; assigning another family member to attend in your stead does not make up for your absence.

There were times during my children's teenage years when I felt like I didn't have a life—but I did! I had a busy, meaningful existence strengthened by the necessity to frequent the events that were important to my children.

Your presence at the activities that your children are involved in during the teen years is the loudest and most affirmative "I love you" that you will ever speak.

For those of you who still have children or teenagers at home, take a moment regularly to enjoy your remaining time together. Those days will be gone in the blink of an eye.

—Dr. James Dobson

Stains

Let me tell you something that you probably don't want to hear: your teenager is not perfect and will probably make errors in judgment during these tenuous years. Your incredible adolescent will not make all A's, may not be a starting player on every team, will talk back to you from time to time, will be impatient with siblings, and will even break curfew. But as the mom and as the keeper of the keys of the laundry room, it is up to you to walk them through their weaknesses and blunders with grace and guidance.

MOM, IT'S UP TO YOU TO WALK YOUR TEENS THROUGH THEIR WEAKNESSES AND BLUNDERS WITH GRACE AND GUIDANCE.

I will admit that I overreacted to these teenage faux pas more than I should have. That out-of-control laundry room should have had a sign that read, "This too shall pass." If you can hold your emotions in check and choose to respond rather than react, you will be much closer to erasing the stains of failure and inappropriate behavior. If you can speak with a teen calmly and with loving firmness, the understanding and the coaching that you communicate will make a lasting difference. If you scream, yell, and over-discipline, your child will likely retreat and you will be building a wall rather than a bridge.

A gentle answer turns away wrath, but a harsh word stirs up anger.
—Proverbs 15:1

You must deal with a stain in life the same way you deal with a laundry stain: quickly. Don't allow an issue to simmer for days and do not allow a misstep to go unnoticed or ignored. When you know that your teen has made a poor choice, deal with it swiftly and thoroughly. Again, recognize the fact that you don't have a perfect child and that we are all sinners in need of grace. Dole out appropriate punishment based on fairness rather than overreacting. I have been guilty of reacting emotionally and telling a child something like this:

- You will never eat dessert again as long as you live in this house!

- You will never be allowed to drive the car until you are twenty-one!

- I will never give you an allowance again!

Generally, when the chief laundress—that is you, dear mom—uses the word *never* in trying to wipe out a stain, the punishment will not last and you will have to retract your words. When one of my teens made a serious error in his or her behavior, I would often ask what he or she thought that the punishment should be in response to the misstep. I found that they came up with discipline that was often much more harsh than I would have meted out.

Wash me thoroughly from my guilt and cleanse me from my sin.
—Psalm 51:2

As the mother, you must speak with your children at a young age about moral purity. This is one conversation that you don't want to put off until it is too late. Truthfully, the discussion about sexual feelings and moral purity should ideally begin before their twelfth birthday, depending on their maturity level. I wish that this topic were as easily covered as when I was a teenager. Today, our teens face the issues of pornography, sexting, gay and transgender acceptance, and "gender fluidity."

If you have the Internet, you have opened the door in your home to easily access the smut and erotica of our culture. If your child has a cell phone, you are giving them the ability to send and receive sexually explicit text messages and photos. Even secular studies show that parents should delay giving their child a phone as long as possible for this very reason.

 YOUR JOB IS TO INTERVENE IN THE LIVES OF YOUR CHILDREN AND BEGIN THE CONVERSATION ABOUT MORAL PURITY AND THE DANGERS OF PORN AT AN EARLY AGE.

Your job is to intervene in the lives of your children and begin the conversation about moral purity and the dangers of pornography at an early age. One conversation is not enough; you must be willing to talk to your son or daughter often about this very difficult subject. Institute absolute protocol in your home for using the Internet, computers, television, and smart phones. One of the most important investments you can make is to place a filtering and reporting program on these devices. All computers and screens should be required to stay in the kitchen or family room so that it becomes difficult to hide what is being viewed. We mandated that all smart phones were to be plugged in for recharging in the kitchen at 10 p.m. and could be retrieved the next morning at breakfast.

It is also vital that you share with your teens the great reward of moral purity and how wonderful sex can be within a marriage. It is extremely appropriate to teach your teens that sex was God's idea and that when we experience it within His boundaries, it is a gift of intimacy and excitement. However, when sex is cheapened through experiences outside of marriage, it becomes a life-threatening trap. Study the Scriptures together when your child is still a young teen and show your adolescent what God has to say about the beautiful gift of sex.

Purify me with hyssop, and I will be clean; cleanse me, and I shall be whiter than snow.   —Psalm 51:7

14

The Prayer Closet

*Do not be afraid, for I am with you; I will bring your children from
the east and gather you from the west. I will say to the north, "Give
them up!" and to the south, "Do not hold them back." Bring my sons
from afar and my daughters from the ends of the earth—everyone
who is called by my name, whom I created for my glory, whom I
formed and made.* —Isaiah 43:5–7 NIV

The prayer closet of your heart is a quiet place yet it is a room of unmatched
power and unyielding purpose. Your greatest battles as a mother will be fought
and will be won in the prayer closet of your heart. If you refuse to spend time
there, you will always be frustrated, always be impatient, and always be deny-
ing your children the greatest gift you can give to them. When you diligently
and faithfully pray for your children, your prayers become the conduit through
which God's power and His blessing are delivered to your children's lives.

Will you pray?

Prayer does not fit us for the greater work; prayer is the greater
work. —Oswald Chambers

A child whose mother prays has inherited a greater endowment than an Ivy League education offers, than a successful family business ensures, or a million dollar inheritance provides. Your prayers will live beyond your life and will follow your children for decades to come. In the heart of a mother, the call to prayer should be louder and more compelling than the call to shop, socialize, or exercise. You must prioritize prayer—you simply must. You must spend hours of time in this restorative and persuasive corner of your heart; in this place, you will take mighty territory for the kingdom of God through your children's lives.

Will you pray?

The greatest parenting resource you have been given is the resource of prayer. When you pray, you will ascertain that your child is in the heart and hands of the One who created them before the foundation of the world. When you pray, you can be assured that the One who cares the most is working behind the scenes to perform a miracle.

Will you pray?

Your child is a tangible demonstration of God's great love for you and His blessing in your life, whether He gave this child to you biologically, through adoption, or through fostering. Each child is a profound and unmatched treasure placed under your spiritual authority for the rest of his or her life. As you read this chapter, surrender your precious child back to God and allow Him to fill you with His limitless strength.

Will you pray?

It is your God-given right as a believer in Jesus Christ to approach the throne room of God boldly.

Let us therefore come boldly to the throne of grace, that we may obtain mercy and find grace to help in time of need.

—Hebrews 4:16 NKJV

When you come boldly into the presence of the Father, He will be there to help you and listen to your concerns as a mother. Tell Him fearlessly what your needs are and what your children's needs are. He wants to know! He longs to hear your heart and partner with you in the daunting assignment of motherhood.

GOD THE FATHER LONGS TO HEAR YOUR HEART AND PARTNER WITH YOU IN THE DAUNTING ASSIGNMENT OF MOTHERHOOD.

This is a glorious and eternal purpose! As a believer and as a mother, your job assignment is to ask of the Father. He has committed in His Word to give you what you and your child need according to His perfect will.

Will you pray?

This is the confidence which we have before Him, that, if we ask anything according to His will, He hears us. And if we know that He hears us in whatever we ask, we know that we have the requests which we have asked from Him. —1 John 5:14–15

You're Having a Baby!

From the instant that you discover that there is a little life growing in your womb, begin to pray for this child who is known by the Father. If you are a single mom, gather others around you to pray with you and for your child. If you are married, every evening before you go to bed, lay your hands on your womb with your husband and pray for this sweet little life you have been given by the Creator of all life. It is during these days when your baby is growing and developing in your womb that the practice of praying Scriptures over your child begins.

For You created my innermost parts; You wove me in my mother's womb. I will give thanks to You, because I am awesomely and wonderfully made; wonderful are Your works, and my soul knows it very well. My frame was not hidden from You when I was made in secret, and skillfully formed in the depths of the earth; Your eyes have seen my formless substance; and in Your book were written all the days

that were ordained for me, when as yet there was not one of them.
—Psalm 139:13–16

Perhaps this child is a *surprise* and you feel that your life has been interrupted. I can assure you that there are no surprises to the Father's heart and certainly no accidents in the kingdom of God. If your baby is a surprise to your well-made plans and your heart is in turmoil, it is vital that you pray and surrender your life to the plans and purposes of God:

> Father, I love You and I know that Your ways are higher than mine. I surrender my time and my plans to You. I know that Your plans are always good and that You are well able to work all things together for good. I ask You to give me a deep and unconditional love for the baby who is growing inside of me. I ask You to do great things through this little one's life in the years to come. I declare today, just as Mary did so many years ago, *"Behold the maidservant of the Lord! Let it be to me according to your word"* (Luke 1:38 NKJV). In Jesus's name I pray. Amen.

If your pregnancy has been planned for and even longed for, prayers of celebration and acceptance will joyfully flow around the life of the wee one who is growing inside of you. Pray for your child's health and his or her childhood friends and future spouse:

> Jesus, I'm having a baby! Thank You for entrusting me with this significant little life. I pray that You will knit this child together in my womb and that my baby will be healthy and strong all the days of their life. I pray that even now You are preparing my child's spouse and that they will serve You together with their whole hearts. I pray for my child's friends through the years; send them friends who will encourage them to follow You. Lord, send my child friends who will be kind and fun. Thank You, Father, for this baby. You are so good to me!

Pray that a spirit of wisdom will guide your precious child and that your child will jump for joy in your womb like John the Baptist did. Pray that your son or daughter will come to know Jesus at an early age and that they will be submissive and obedient, especially during the teenage and young adult years:

Jesus, I pray for my unborn yet so loved child today. I pray that even now, even in my womb, that a spirit of wisdom will rest upon my child. I pray that like You, my child will grow *"in wisdom and stature, and in favor with God and man"* (Luke 2:52 NIV). I pray that You will guide my child in all of his or her choices in life. I pray that this child will come to know You at an early age and will surrender his or her life completely to You! I pray that my son or daughter will make God-honoring decisions as a teenager and young adult. Father, would You put a hunger in my child for Your Word? Use this little one as part of Your strategy for the next generation in Your unshakable kingdom, Father! In Jesus's name I pray. Amen.

I remember my mother's prayers and they have always followed me. They have clung to me all my life.   —Abraham Lincoln

Preschool Prayers

When you are completely worn out and at the end of your endurance over toddler antics and the unending energy that is abundant in your wee one, that is probably when you need to pray the most! You will never make it through the preschool years if you are relying upon your own strength and ingenuity. You need to pray more than you need chocolate, more than you need a day at the spa, or even more than you need a night of uninterrupted sleep:

Jesus, I need Your help! I need Your strength and Your power. I need You to overwhelm me with Your patience and with Your peace. Would You give me everything that I need to face this day and to love this child? Would You give me creativity and joy as I shepherd this little one for Your kingdom? In Jesus's name I pray. Amen.

Prayers of protection are needful at every season in your child's life but especially during the preschool years when their bodies are energetic and their brains are immature:

Lord, would You protect my little one today? Would You protect him/her from fevers, colds, and contagious diseases? I thank You that You have given Your angels charge concerning my child in all of his/her ways. I pray that my child will have no broken bones, require no stitches, and experience no injuries that present long-term damage. Thank You, Father, for loving my child more than I ever could. You are a good, good Father. In Jesus's name I pray. Amen.

But the Lord is faithful, and He will strengthen and protect you from the evil one. —2 Thessalonians 3:3

Friends, Bullies, and "Things that Go Bump in the Night"

 YOU MUST DILIGENTLY WATCH WHO IS INFLUENCING YOUR CHILD'S LIFE AND GUARD THEM FROM UNNECESSARY SOCIAL PAIN.

As your child grows into the elementary and middle school years, it's of utmost importance to pray for his or her friends. Friends have the capacity to either wound a child deeply or to greatly encourage. You, as the mom, must diligently watch who is influencing your child's life and guard them from unnecessary social pain; one of the chief ways that you are called to do this is in the prayer closet of your heart:

Lord, I pray that You will choose specific friends for my child. I pray that those who would lead them astray either spiritually or emotionally will not be part of their daily world. I pray that You would send them a friend who loves You deeply and who is an encouragement in all ways to my child. I also pray that You would send my child as an encouragement to someone else. Thank You that my child just might be the answer to another mother's prayer. In Jesus's name I pray. Amen.

If your child is experiencing social distress at school or in the neighborhood, teach your son or daughter to pray and call out to God for His intervention in his or her life. Pray with your child about the challenge that he or she is facing and assess the situation often.

One of the most important prayer assignments that a mother has is praying against fear and anxiety in her child's life. The world is a foreboding place for our children; they often feel overwhelmed at requirements, bullies, entertainment, and social situations. From a very young age, children are afraid that they will not be liked by their peers or recognized by their teachers. How wonderful to know that my prayers, as a mother, are able to chase away the fears simmering in the heart of my child and then to usher in an attitude of peace and confidence!

Jesus, I thank You that You have not given my child a spirit of fear but of power, love, and a sound mind. I thank You that in Your name, no weapon formed against my child will prosper. I bind a spirit of fear and I loosen a spirit of peace, wholeness, and well-being in the spirit and in the soul of my precious child. I pray that when my child lays his/her head down on the pillow at night that he/she will sleep peacefully and You will minister to this tender child even then. In Jesus's name I pray. Amen.

If you are a stranger to prayer, you are a stranger to the greatest source of power known to human beings.   —Billy Sunday

Help! I Have a Teenager!

The middle school years and the teenage years can be the most exasperating times of a mother's life...or they can be the most delightful. I believe that prayer is able to lay the groundwork to turn the frustrations into fun. A mother who prays diligently for her teenager is that child's greatest gift, although they may not realize it at the time. If you pray earnestly, listen attentively, speak kindly, and love unconditionally, the teen years may be your favorite years of parenting the flock you have been given by the Father!

One of the main focuses of prayer during the teenage years is for their self-esteem. Teens are bullied by comparisons in the world of academics, athletics, peers, and appearance.

> Lord, I thank You that my son/daughter has been fearfully and wonderfully made by You and that You don't make mistakes! Father, I pray that my child will see himself/herself in the way that You do. I pray that Your Holy Spirit will encourage my child daily and he/she will be stamped with Your identity! In Jesus's name I pray. Amen.

If you have prayed with your child during the formative years of life, you have a greater possibility of praying with your teenager without too much resistance. Until they went off to college, I continued to pray with my children before they left for school in the morning and at bedtime. The prayers were not long but they were meaningful and targeted. For example, I would pray:

> Father, I pray that You will be with Matthew today. Thank You that You are guiding his steps everywhere he goes and that You are the One who is giving favor to my son. I pray that he will carry honor with him and make wise choices in the midst of this day. Give him words to speak that are encouraging. Help him to work diligently and faithfully in all that he does. In Jesus's name I pray. Amen.

I firmly believe that one of the most important prayers you can pray during the teen years is for moral purity in the life of your child. It is inevitable that your son or daughter will begin to be interested in the opposite sex during these years. A mother's prayers are able to channel those desires and deliver wisdom despite the sex-driven culture in which we live.

Father, I pray that You will guide and guard my child's raging hormones. I pray for his/her mind, that he/she will think pure thoughts, and will take every other thought captive to the obedience of Your Son. I pray that You will give my child the tenacity to say *no* to what is sin and *yes* to what is pure. Father, I pray that You would keep my child pure until his/her wedding night. In Jesus's name I pray. Amen.

The prayer that stirred deeply within my soul during the teen years was one of purpose and calling in the lives of each of my dearly loved but quickly departing children. A mother must pray for doors to open, decisions to be made, and purpose to be revealed.

Father, I thank You that my child is part of Your creative genius for this generation. Thank You for stirring up each gift, talent, and ability that You placed within the soul of my child since the beginning of time. I pray that You will open the right doors and close the wrong doors. I pray that You will send men and women into my child's life to help him/her with direction and purpose. Once again, Father, I surrender my child to You and ask that You would use him/her mightily for kingdom purposes. In Jesus's name I pray. Amen.

"For I know the plans that I have for you," declares the Lord, *"plans for prosperity and not for disaster, to give you a future and a hope."*
—Jeremiah 29:11

You've Only Just Begun

When your children have left the family home for college, or a career, or to establish a family of their own, your time in the prayer closet of your heart has only just begun! Your young adult children can run from your words but they can never escape your prayers, so your strategy should be to pray more and talk less!

Father, I thank You that You allowed me to raise this child for Your kingdom. I pray in Jesus's mighty name that You would protect, guide, and guard my child. I pray for divine appointments and a wisdom that transcends common sense. Lead my child into all righteousness and into living wholeheartedly for Your Son and His kingdom. In Jesus's name I pray. Amen.

Every great movement of God can be traced to a kneeling figure.
—D. L. Moody

15

The Front Porch

The LORD will give strength to His people; the LORD will bless His people with peace. —Psalm 29:11

How many times is it possible for a mother to say goodbye without having her heart irretrievably smashed into a million broken pieces?

How many times will I stand on the front porch with my heart uncontrollably splashing down my cheeks?

It all began in August 1999, when our oldest son Matthew drove away in his burgundy Jeep Grand Cherokee to begin his freshman year at a Christian university thousands of miles from home. His secondhand vehicle, purchased by his generous grandparents, was packed to the roof with sheets, towels, pillows, a comforter, luggage, a wastepaper basket, a laundry basket, books, pictures, and everything and anything else a young man eighteen years old could possibly need as he left his mom and his childhood home. His dad was driving across the country with him and they were both literally euphoric with excitement and anticipation.

You know how boys are—they can't wait to be independent and their dads cheer them on. You also know how moms are—they want to hold on just a minute or two longer.

They were giddy while I was grieving.

Gathered on the front porch with me were both of Matt's grandmothers, his four younger siblings, and the family dog. I don't know who cried louder—me, his five-year-old sister, or his grandmothers. Even the dog was wailing mournfully.

We stood on the front porch as they drove down our long driveway, honking the horn and waving their arms out of the windows until I could no longer see or hear them. My tears flooded my cheeks and I thought that my heart would never heal. Even now, as I write this over twenty years later, the tears of motherhood are dripping on my computer keys.

Did I say everything that I wanted to say?

Did I do a good job?

What would I do differently if I had it to do all over again?

This was the day that I had dreaded for eighteen and a half years. Ever since Dr. Hanes had laid Matt in my arms, I had the silent foreboding that someday this child would leave me. *Where had the years gone?*

I remember thinking, *My number is up. Millions of women have done this over the course of history. Millions of women have let their children grow up and leave home. And now it is my turn. I hate taking my turn.*

As I was sobbing in a very unattractive manner, my very sensitive ten-year-old son piped up, "Well, Mom, at least you are not sending him off to war."

I cried louder.

Goodbye?! Oh, no, please! Can't we go back to page one and do it
all over again?   —Winnie the Pooh

The First Lesson From the Front Porch

Our children don't belong to us; they are on loan from the Father. What a glorious arrangement between God and mothers! For eighteen years, we are called to partner with heaven in raising a man or a woman for the kingdom of

God. We have not been called upon to *own* the children we have been given but we have been asked to *raise* them. When you raise something, it implies a beginning and an end.

FOR EIGHTEEN YEARS, WE ARE CALLED TO PARTNER WITH HEAVEN IN RAISING A MAN OR A WOMAN FOR THE KINGDOM OF GOD.

From the moment of my children's births, I prepared myself for this moment. I knew that it would be hard but I also knew that they couldn't live with me forever. It was inevitable for them to seek independence and grow into their destinies in Christ. God has called us, as mothers, to prepare for the eventual goodbyes in life.

It is a step-by-step process but each step prepares us for the final goodbye. There comes a day when a nursing baby stops nursing and graduates to the sippy cup. There comes a day when a baby who has loved to be carried decides that it is time to walk. There comes a day when children no longer want to be read to but learn how to read for themselves. All of those experiences become part of the *front porch* of a mother's heart.

Learn to love the moments when you are preparing a human to be part of the greater plan of God. It's a historic opportunity for a woman to be an integral part of God's solution to a dark world. You have been invited by the Creator to send out warriors and champions. You have been commissioned by the Father of all humanity to send light-bearers into darkness and righteous soldiers into evil. Your job, should you choose to accept it, is to develop a tiny mass of humanity into a mountain-moving, earth-shaking, Red Sea-parting threat to the kingdom of darkness.

These future men and women are not yours but are His. Release them gladly and cheer for them loudly. It's what mothers do on the front porch of their hearts.

Two Years Later

Two short years later, it was time for Christopher to leave home and attend that same Christian university thousands of miles away. The night before he was to leave the family nest, I was sitting in my chair in my bedroom, reading my Bible. This particular chair and my well-worn Bible had accompanied me through many joys and sorrows in life. I sat in this chair to pray for my children and to choose joy when depression had consumed me. I had sat in this same chair every early morning hour when I just needed more of Jesus to get through the day. This chair had embraced me at the end of every long day when I was desperate for strength and comfort.

Christopher was leaving me in the morning. The little boy with the contagious grin, sparkling blue eyes, and a song in his heart had grown into a fine young man. He was ready...but I was not. I did the only thing that I knew to do as my heart was heaving with yet another goodbye: I prayed and I read my Bible in my familiar yet tattered chair.

My dire prayer that August evening was, "Lord, I want to make it through this. If You will give me a Bible verse that I can stand on, I will be okay. Please, Lord, speak to me through Your Word." And honestly, I added an addendum to that mournful plea, "Lord, if You don't give me a Scripture, I am not going to make it, so You better show up!"

In the stillness of the moment, I heard Him whisper to me, "Read Isaiah 33:6."

I was forty-six and this was only the second time in my life that I heard the voice of God directing me to a specific passage in Scripture. With a tissue in one hand and my Bible in the other, I hastily turned to Isaiah 33:6: *"And He will be the stability of your times, a wealth of salvation, wisdom, and knowledge; the fear of the Lord is his treasure."*

YOUR STABILITY, YOUR SECURITY, AND YOUR STRENGTH COME FROM THE LORD—NOT FROM YOUR CHILDREN.

What a gift! What an absolute gift from the throne room of God to this mother's ravaged heart! The Lord was reminding me that my stability, my security, and my strength came from Him—not from my children. My wealth did not come from the family that Craig and I had created but it had come from the Lord. Although I was still grieving over the upcoming departure of

Christopher from our home, I knew that I had now been given the benefit of the steadfast power of the Lord.

Early the next morning, we reenacted the same scene from just two years earlier. Christopher Burton McLeod, accompanied by his dad, was about to drive away in his silver Oldsmobile Alero, packed to the ceiling with stuff that I thought he needed. I stood at the door of the home that used to house a mom, a dad, five incredible kids, and a dog. We were down to a mom, a dad, and three incredible kids. Even the family dog was no longer with us.

Where had the years gone? Why did the childhood years evaporate into thin air? How could these brilliant, talented, adorable kids that I had given birth to and then raised have the nerve to leave me?

Although the questions of goodbye were still boiling in my heart, this time, I had the strength to wisely answer each one.

Never say goodbye, because saying goodbye means going away and going away means forgetting.   —Peter Pan

The Second Lesson From the Porch

Are you ready for the most difficult lesson that a mother learns on the front porch of her heart? It may cause you to recoil in emotional pain but the faster that you learn this lesson, the healthier that your relationships will be with your grown children.

I have learned that the more I hang on to my grown children, the more that I lose them; conversely, the more that I allow them to be independent, the more that I have them. So, uncurl your fingers from the grip on your grown children and cheer for them from a distance. The welcome mat will always be out on the front porch for these pieces of your heart who have somehow found a way to live autonomously from you. Allow them the dignity of growing away from the family home. You will give yourself a gift if you truly allow them to be strong, vital individuals who are living the life that God has for them rather than the life Mom has for them.

Never place undue pressure on them to come home but let them know that they are always welcome. Do not make them feel guilty for spending days or holidays with their spouse's family but let them know that you will look forward to seeing them in the future.

I have also learned in the years of observing my children as young adults that they can run away from my words but they can never escape my prayers, so my strategy is to pray more and talk less. It's a lesson that is only learned on the front porch of a mother's heart.

 NEVER PLACE UNDUE PRESSURE ON YOUR CHILDREN TO COME HOME BUT LET THEM KNOW THAT THEY ARE ALWAYS WELCOME.

One by One

One by one, they have left me standing there.

Jordan, that little boy with the infectious giggle and never-ending energy, left for college just before he turned eighteen. He had the nerve to be happy about leaving me! All I could ask myself was, "Where have eighteen summers, eighteen birthdays, and eighteen Christmases gone?"

Joy, the daughter who always lived up to her name, left two years later. She was the little girl who had danced her way into everyone's heart and filled our home with music. Her absence left a lingering fragrance in a nearly empty home.

Four short years later, the baby, Joni Rebecca, who had come to us later in life, decided to attend that same Christian university halfway across the country. There is no pain so real and raw as the pain of a mother saying good-bye to the last one.

Now what will I do? Now who will I be? These were the questions that echoed through the canyons of my deserted heart.

There was one more question that I was audacious enough to ask the Father, "Will I ever do anything again as significant as being a mom? Will I?"

I don't do transition well. As a human, I deeply desired for my life to stay the same. As a mother, I didn't really want my children to age; I wanted them all to be about ten years old and eat a nutritious, home-cooked meal at my dinner table every night. *Why can't little girls keep giggling and dancing? Is there a law against little boys staying little? Why must we add a candle every year to a child's birthday cake?*

There is one eternal, simple yet ravaging answer to those questions: "It's the plan of God for children to grow up and leave." God has called every human being to grow up and go; your children don't receive a pass just because you are their mom. We serve a God who loves to see His baby birds flutter their as yet untried wings and then begin to soar into their destinies. Although we serve a God who never changes, we serve a God who loves to stir up change.

WE SERVE A GOD WHO LOVES TO SEE HIS CHILDREN LEAVE THEIR NESTS AND SOAR INTO THEIR DESTINIES.

God's plan has always been a plan of birth, of growing into maturity, of changing with the seasons, of saying goodbye, and of beginning again.

We serve a God who makes all things new and whose perfect plan is that our security is to be in Him and not in others. We serve a God who loves the family unit but who does not want the members of that precious group of people to replace Him on the throne of their hearts.

I believe that God stands on the front porch of our hearts with every brokenhearted mother and even holds us as we say goodbye. I also believe that He is smiling while I am sobbing. God treasures and encourages each goodbye we are forced to say. God gives people to us for a lifetime but He gives Himself to us for all of eternity. God gives children to us for a season but He gives Himself in limitless relationship.

Don't cry because it's over, smile because it happened.

—Dr. Seuss

Waiting on the Front Porch

These days, when my doorbell rings, I often find a package on the front porch that has been delivered due to an order that I placed. These packages have been carefully selected and purchased; when one appears on our front porch, I open it with great anticipation and excitement. *Is what's inside the package the same as my order?*

Parenting is a bit different than the process of selecting, paying for, and then opening an expected item.

In the years of the empty nest, as I relax on the front porch of mothering, the packages that I am examining contain the reality of how my children have turned out. I prayerfully inspect the lives that they are living as young adults and I realize, with tears and with pain, that I wish some of them were making different choices with the life that they have been given. I wonder if I could have done something different, if I could have impacted their lives in a more meaningful manner, and if I was enough as the mother of each beloved child.

IN MOMENTS OF TEARS AND DISAPPOINTMENT, THE LORD HAS BEEN FAITHFUL TO MEET ME ON THE FRONT PORCH AND SIT WITH ME AWHILE.

In those moments of tears and even disappointment, the Lord has been faithful to meet me on the front porch and sit with me awhile. He has assured me that we are not given the assignment of motherhood to ensure a perfect product or to spit out cookie-cutter children but we are asked to do it as unto Him. We, as mothers, are prodded to joyfully sacrifice the years of our lives and offer them on the altar of His call and His purposes.

For the mother whose children no longer live in the family home, the front porch becomes a place of surrender and miracles. Just as the father of the prodigal son demonstrated 2,000 years ago, I am waiting on the front porch in intrepid faith and with immutable hope. I continue to love my children with an unconditional and even defiant love. I will declare the promises found in the Word of God over the lives of all of my children and will be a warrior mom who destroys the plans of the enemy with uncommon valor and bravery. I pray:

Lord, Your Word says that when we train up a child in the way he should go, even when he is old, he will not depart from it. (Proverbs 22:6.) Although I wasn't a perfect mom, I was a mom who taught my children to love You so I thank You that my child is coming back in Jesus's name! I thank You that he/she will return to Your ways and to Your calling! In the miraculous name of Jesus, I pray. Amen!

Lord, I pray that You will enlighten the eyes of my child's heart and that he/she will know the hope of Your calling and the riches of the glory of Your inheritance in the saints. (Ephesians 1:18.) In Jesus's name, I pray. Amen.

Lord, I pray that just like the prodigal son came to his senses that my son/daughter will come to their senses wherever he/she is and whatever he/she is doing. (Luke 15:17.) In Jesus's name, I pray. Amen.

I will not give up in prayer and I will stay firmly seated on the front porch until all are safely home. And when that day comes, we will celebrate with open arms and unconditional love!

This is what the LORD *says: "Restrain your voice from weeping and your eyes from tears; for your work will be rewarded," declares the* LORD, *"and they will return from the land of the enemy. There is hope for your future," declares the* LORD, *"and your children will return to their own territory."* —Jeremiah 31:16–17

The Final Lesson From the Front Porch

Now that my children have been adults for many years, I have learned that I still have oversight in their lives. As the one who continues to love each one with great tenderness and unconditional support, I am called to be their chief prayer warrior. I may not be fixing their meals any longer but I am still impacting their spiritual and mental health by the prayers that I pray. I may no longer be tucking them into their small beds but I can protect them through the shield of prayer. And, truly, if we believe the tenets of our faith, we will realize that this season is perhaps a more powerful season than the one of tying shoes, fixing boo-boos, and reading bedtime stories.

EVEN WHEN YOU ARE NO LONGER TUCKING YOUR CHILDREN INTO THEIR BEDS, YOU CAN PROTECT THEM THROUGH THE SHIELD OF PRAYER.

Each year during the week between Christmas and New Year's Day, I still ask the Lord to give a Scripture to me for each child for the coming year. As I pray and ponder over the Word and listen for the leading of the Holy Spirit, I am always led to specific verses for each child and their spouse.

This year, for my daughter who is struggling with infertility, I have been praying, "Lord, I thank You that Your Word says that You make the barren woman abide in the house *'as a joyful mother of children'* (Psalm 113:9). Praise the Lord!"

For my oldest son Matt, who is a high school varsity basketball coach and also helps to lead a national sports organization, I have prayed, "Lord, I thank You that Matt is a noble man. Your Word says that the noble man makes noble plans *'and by noble plans he stands'* (Isaiah 32:8)."

Now that the years of a mountain of laundry, Easter egg hunts, and ballet recitals are passed, you still have an enormous job as a mother. It is on the front porch of your heart that you are commissioned to be a prayer warrior that makes hell shake and heaven applaud!

Hear my prayer, LORD, listen to my pleadings! Answer me in Your faithfulness, in Your righteousness. —Psalm 143:1

Goodbye in Any Language

There are many languages spoken on the front porch of a mother's heart... and goodbye is the dreaded word spoken there. Why is this word so hideously agonizing for us?

Goodbye... Adieu... Farewell... Adiós... See ya later, alligator... Auf Wiedersehen... Au revoir... Ciao... Sayōnara...

You can say *goodbye* a thousand different ways in a myriad of languages but I will never like its meaning. The seven inconsequential letters of *goodbye* have broken my heart too many times to count.

Although I am not an expert on the Icelandic language, I did discover that in this particular tongue, the word for *bless* is used to say goodbye. Oh! My empty heart is being healed even with the thought that I don't have to say goodbye but what I must do is *bless* my children on their life's journey. The blessing of a mother can never be underestimated or ignored. A mother's blessing is one of the most lasting gifts we can give to our children.

As you stand on the front porch of your heart and prepare to send your children into the great unknown, rather than say goodbye with tears and gulping sobs, you can say, "Bless" with joy and anticipation!

Now may the God of hope fill you with all joy and peace in believing,
so that you will abound in hope by the power of the Holy Spirit.
—Romans 15:13

As I was thinking about the different ways to say goodbye, I recalled a song that my high school choir sang on graduation day:

Shalom, shalom,
You'll find shalom
The nicest greeting you know;
It means bonjour, salud, and skoal
And twice as much as hello.
It means a million lovely things,
Like peace be yours,
Welcome home.
And even when you say goodbye,
You say goodbye with shalom.
It's a very useful word,
It can get you through the day;
All you really need to know,
You can hardly go wrong,
This is your home as long as you say:

Shalom,
The nicest greeting I know;
Shalom,
Means twice as much as hello.
It means a million lovely things,
Like peace be yours,
Welcome home.

And even when you say goodbye,
If your voice has
"I don't want to go" in it,
Say goodbye with a little "hello" in it,
And say goodbye with shalom.[8]

What a lovely thought! When we declare *shalom*—the Hebrew word for *peace*—over our children, we are blessing their coming and their going. *Shalom* is a declaration of living a complete life free from frustration and confusion; it is a blessing of tranquility, peace, and friendship.

THE BENEDICTION OF SHALOM NOT ONLY IMPLIES PEACE FROM WAR BUT ALSO PEACE IN HUMAN RELATIONSHIPS AND PEACE WITH GOD IN A COVENANT RELATIONSHIP.

The benediction of *shalom* not only implies peace from war but also peace in human relationships and peace with God in a covenant relationship. As I have allowed the eternal meaning of shalom to penetrate my heart, I have decided to have it inscribed on a beautiful plaque and then to hang it over my front porch as a reminder that when I don't want to say *goodbye*, I can simply say, "Shalom!"

Smiling From the Front Porch

The pain of goodbye never gets easier, although it does become more familiar. As I stood outside the security area at the airport while sending our youngest daughter off for her final semester in college, I sobbed uncontrollably.

8. "Shalom" by Jerry Herman, for the 1961 Broadway musical *Milk and Honey.*

She kept looking back at me to make sure that I was going to be fine. I wasn't fine and I never would be fine again but somehow I would find the strength that I needed.

However, as Joni made it through security and turned around one last time, she saw a smile on my face. I was waving frantically and cheering her on. "Have a great semester, honey! I'll see you before you know it!"

As I reached my car in the airport parking lot, I blew my nose one last time, stuffed the tissue in my pocket, and wiped the dripping mascara off my cheek.

I put my car in drive and forced myself not to look in the rearview mirror.

The front porch is where a mother chooses to begin again and where she prays for new and divine purpose. The front porch is a place of increased adventures and greater callings. An empty nest is not nearly so empty when a weeping mother allows God to fill up every corner of every room of her heart.

This is the moment for which you were created, dear mom! You were created for the front porch!

The Hand that Rocks the Cradle

by William Ross Wallace (1819–1881)

Blessings on the hand of women!
Angels guard its strength and grace,
In the palace, cottage, hovel,
Oh, no matter where the place;
Would that never storms assailed it,
Rainbows ever gently curled,
For the hand that rocks the cradle
Is the hand that rules the world.

Infancy's the tender fountain,
Power may with beauty flow,
Mother's first to guide the streamlets,
From them souls unresting grow—
Grow on for the good or evil,
Sunshine streamed or evil hurled;

For the hand that rocks the cradle
Is the hand that rules the world.

Woman, how divine your mission
Here upon our natal sod!
Keep, oh, keep the young heart open
Always to the breath of God!
All true trophies of the ages
Are from mother-love impearled;
For the hand that rocks the cradle
Is the hand that rules the world.

Blessings on the hand of women!
Fathers, sons, and daughters cry,
And the sacred song is mingled
With the worship in the sky—
Mingles where no tempest darkens,
Rainbows evermore are hurled;
For the hand that rocks the cradle
Is the hand that rules the world.

APPENDIX A
Books for Every Age and Stage

Books for the Baby

Baby Bear Sees Blue by Ashley Wolff
Barnyard Dance! by Sandra Boynton
Bunny Cakes by Rosemary Wells
Chicka Chicka Boom Boom by Bill Martin Jr. and John Archambault
Corduroy by Don Freeman
Go to Sleep, Little Farm by Mary Lyn Ray
Goodnight, Moon by Margaret Wise Brown and Clement Hurd
I Am a Bunny by Ole Risom and Richard Scarry
I Love You to the Moon and Back by Amelia Hepworth and Tim Warnes
Little Bear's Little Boat by Eve Bunting
Little Blue Truck Books by Alice Schertle, illustrated by Jill McElmurry
Little Poems for Tiny Ears by Lin Oliver and Tomie dePaola
Llama Llama Red Pajama by Anna Dewdney
My Blue Boat by Chris L. Demarest
On the Night You Were Born by Nancy Tillman
Owl Babies by Martin Waddell
Pat the Bunny by Dorothy Kunhardt
Prayer for a Child by Rachel Field
Sheep in a Jeep by Nancy E. Shaw and Margot Apple
The Little Rabbit by Judy Dunn
Where Do Diggers Sleep at Night? by Brianna Caplan Sayres and Christian Slade
Where's Spot by Eric Hill
Yellow Ball by Molly Bang

> Books are not made for furniture, but there is nothing else that
> so beautifully furnishes a house.   —Henry Ward Beecher

Books for Toddlers and Preschoolers; Picture Books

A Blue Butterfly by Bijou Le Tord

A Butterfly Is Patient by Dianna Hutts Aston and Sylvia Long

A Seed Is Sleeping by Dianna Hutts Aston and Sylvia Long

A Tree Is Nice by Janice May Udry and Marc Simont

All the World by Liz Garton Scanlon and Marla Frazee

Alphabears by Kathleen and Michael Hague

An Egg Is Quiet by Dianna Hutts Aston and Sylvia Long

Any book illustrated by Eloise Wilkin

Are You My Mother? by P.D. Eastman

Ask Mr. Bear by Marjorie Flack

Baby Dear by Esther and Eloise Wilkin

Big Red Barn by Margaret Wise Brown

Blueberries for Sal by Robert McCloskey

Brown Bear, Brown Bear, What Do You See? by Bill Martin Jr. and Eric Carle

Caps for Sale by Esphyr Slobodkina

Clifford the Big Red Dog series by Norman Bridwell

Curious George books by H. A. Rey and Margret Rey

Giraffes Can't Dance by Giles Andreae

God Bless You and Goodnight by Hannah Hall

Harry by the Sea by Gene Zion and Margaret Bloy Graham

Harry the Dirty Dog by Gene Zion and Margaret Bloy Graham

I'll Never Let You Go by Smriti Prasadam-Halls and Alison Brown

If Jesus Came to My House by Joan G. Thomas, Henri Sorensen, et al.

If You Give a Mouse a Cookie and other books by Laura Numeroff, illustrated by Felicia Bond

In a Blue Room by Jim Averbeck and Tricia Tusa

It Ain't Gonna Rain No More by Karen Beaumont, illustrated by David Catrow

Jesse Bear, What Will You Wear? by Nancy White Carlstrom

Joseph Had a Little Overcoat by Sims Taback

Library Lion by Michelle Knudsen, illustrated by Kevin Hawkes

Little Brown Bear by Elizabeth Norine Upham

Love You Forever by Robert Munsch and Sheila McGraw

Make Way for Ducklings by Robert McCloskey

Mighty, Mighty Construction Site by Sherri Rinker and Ethan Long

Mike Mulligan and His Steamshovel by Virginia Lee Burton

Miss Rumphius by Barbara Coony

My First Mother Goose by Tomie dePaola

My Little Artist by Donna Green

My Mama Had a Dancing Heart by Libba Moore Gray

Noah's Ark by Peter Speier

Officer Buckle and Gloria by Peggy Rathmann

Red Knit Cap Girl and the Reading Tree by Naoko Stoop

Richard Scarry's books

Saint George and the Dragon by Margaret Hodges, illustrated by Trina Schart Hyman

Snow by Uri Schulevitz

The Berenstain Bears series by Stan and Jan Berenstain

The Big Green Pocketbook by Candice F. Ransom and Felicia Bond
The Big Orange Splot by Daniel Pinkwater
The Boy Who Held Back the Sea by Lenny Hort, Thomas Locker, et al.
The First Teddy Bear by Helen Kay, illustrated by Susan Detwiler
The Jesus Storybook Bible by Sally Lloyd-Jones and Jago
The Kissing Hand by Audrey Penn, illustrated by Ruth Harper
The Little Engine that Could by Watty Piper and George and Doris Hauman
The Little Family by Lois Lenski
The Little House by Virginia Lee Burton
The Puppy Who Wanted a Boy by Jane Thayer and Lisa McCue
The Raft by Jim LaMarche
The Rainbow Fish by Marcus Pfister and J. Alison James
The Relatives Came by Cynthia Rylant and Stephen Gammell
The Runaway Bunny by Margaret Wise Brown and Clement Hurd
The Very Hungry Caterpillar by Eric Carle
Toot and Puddle by Holly Hobbie
Toy Boat by Randall de Sève and Loren Long
We're Going on a Bear Hunt by Michael Rosen
When God Made You by Matthew Paul Turner and David Catrow
You're Here for a Reason by Nancy Tillman

A peasant that reads is a prince in waiting.   —Walter Mosely

Early Reader Books

A Pocketful of Goobers by Barbara Mitchell and Peter E. Hanson
A Splash of Red by Jen Bryant and Melissa Sweet
Amber on the Mountain by Tony Johnston and Robert A. Duncan
Andrew Henry's Meadow by Doris Burn
"B" Is for Betsy by Carolyn Haywood
Brave Irene by William Steig
Clara and Davie by Patricia Polacco
Custard the Dragon by Ogden Nash
For Spacious Skies by Olga Baumert and Nancy Churnin
Frog and Toad series by Arnold Lobel
Gramma's Walk by Anna Grossnickle Hines
Grandfather's Journey by Allen Say
Hank the Cowdog series by John R. Erickson, illustrated by Gerald L. Holmes
Harold and the Purple Crayon by Crockett Johnson
Katy and the Big Snow by Virginia Lee Burton
Keep the Lights Burning, Abbie by Connie Roop, Peter Roop, et al.
Linnea's Almanac by Cristina Bjork and Lena Anderson, et al.
Locomotive by Brian Floca
Madeline by Ludwig Bemelmans
Nate the Great by Marjorie Weinman Sharmat and Marc Simont
Nicky the Nature Detective by Ulf Svedberg, Lena Anderson, et al.

On a Beam of Light by Jennifer Berne and Vladimir Radunsky
Ox-Cart Man by Donald Hall, illustrated by Barbara Cooney
Paul Revere's Ride by Henry Wadsworth Longfellow, illustrated by Ted Rand
Pets in a Jar by Seymour Simon and Betty Fraser
Poppleton series by Cynthia Rylant, illustrated by Mark Teague
Rosie's Posies by Marcy Dunn Ramsey
Sam the Minuteman by Nathaniel Benchely and Arnold Lobel
Stopping by the Woods on a Snowy Evening by Robert Frost, illustrated by Susan Jeffers
Storm in the Night by Mary Stolz and Pat Cummings
The Boy Who Loved Math by Deborah Heiligman and LeUyen Pham
The Brave Girl by Michelle Markel and Melissa Sweet
The Curious Garden by Peter Brown
The Fox Went Out on a Chilly Night by Peter Spier
The Gardener by Sarah Stewart, illustrated by David Small
The Gingham Dog and the Calico Cat by Eugene Field
The Keeping Quilt by Patricia Polacco
The Library by Sarah Stewart and David Small
The Life and Times of the Peanut by Charles Micucci
The Long Way to a New Land by Joan Sandin
The Long Way Westward by Joan Sandin
The Matchbox Diary by Paul Fleischman
The Star-Spangled Banner by Peter Spier
The Story About Ping by Marjorie Flack and Kurt Wiese
The Tale of Peter Rabbit by Beatrix Potter
The Wild Horses of Sweetbriar by Natalie Kinsey-Warnock and Ted Rand
They Were Strong and Good by Robert Lawson
Thomas Jefferson Builds a Library by Barb Rosenstock and John O'Brien
Thoughts to Make Your Heart Sing by Sally Lloyd-Jones
Tree Lady by H. Joseph Hopkins and Jill McElmurry
Uncle Jed's Barbershop by Margaree King Mitchell and James E. Ransome
Wagon Wheels by Betty Mermelstein and Cheryl Chan
When I Was Young in the Mountains by Cynthia Rylant and Diane Goode
Who Says Women Can't be Doctors? by Tanya Lee Stone and Marjorie Priceman
You Are Special by Max Lucado, illustrated by Sergio Martinez
Young Teddy Roosevelt by Cheryl Harness

No one can be called friendless who has God and the companionship of good books.
—Elizabeth Barrett Browning

Must-Reads for Elementary Years

A Gathering of Days by Joan Blos
A Long Way from Chicago by Richard Peck
A New Coat for Anna by Harriet Ziefert
A Wrinkle in Time by Madeleine L'Engle
A Year Down Under by Richard Peck

Alexander and the Terrible, Horrible, No Good, Very Bad Day by Judith Viorst, illustrated by Ray Cruz

All of a Kind Family series by Sydney Taylor

Amelia Bedelia series by Peggy Parish

American Girl History Mysteries series by Barbara A. Steiner

Ballet Shoes series by Noel Streatfeild and Diane Goode

Because of Winn Dixie by Kate DiCamillo

Ben and Me: An Astonishing Life of Benjamin Franklin by His Good Mouse Amos by Robert Lawton

Betsy, Tacy series by Maud Hart Lovelace

Bully for You, Teddy Roosevelt! by Jean Fritz and Mike Wimmer

Caddie Woodlawn by Carol Ryrie Brink and Trina Schart

Captain Underpants by Dav Pilkey

Carry on, Mr. Bowditch by Jean Lee Latham

Charlotte's Web by E. B. White

Encyclopedia Brown by Donald J. Sobol

Flat Stanley by Jeff Brown, illustrated by Macky Pamintuan

Frindle by Andrew Clements

From the Mixed-Up Files of Mrs. Basil E. Frankweiler by E.L. Konigsburg

George Washington Carver from "The Heroes of History" series by Janet and Geoff Benge

Hank the Cowdog by John R. Erickson

Heidi by Johanna Spyri

Hitty: Her First Hundred Years by Rachel Field

Homer Price by Robert McCloskey

I Spy Series by Jean Marzollo, illustrated by Walter Wick

In the Year of the Boar and Jackie Robinson by Bette Bao Lord and Marc Simont

Junie B. Jones series by Barbara Park

Just So Stories: for Little Children by Rudyard Kipling

Justin Morgan and the Big Horse Race by Ellen F. Feld

Leonardo's Horse by Jean Fritz and Hudson Talbott

Little Britches by Ralph Moody

Little House on the Prairie series by Laura Ingalls Wilder

Mandy series by Lois Gladys Leppard

Matt Christopher Sports Classics

Misty of Chincoteague by Marguerite Henry

Mr. Popper's Penguins by Richard Atwater, Florence Atwater, et al.

Mrs. Piggle-Wiggle by Betty MacDonald and Alexandra Boiger

Nancy Drew Mystery Stories by Carolyn Keene

Nature Got There First by Phil Gates

North to Freedom by Anne Holm

Peter Pan by J. M. Barrie

Pippy Longstocking by Astrid Lindgren

Pollyanna by Eleanor H. Porter

Ramona Quimby series by Beverly Cleary

Sarah Plain and Tall by Patricia MacLachlan

Shiloh by Phyllis Reynolds Naylor

Skylark by Patricia MacLachlan

Stone Fox by John Reynolds Gardiner and Greg Hargreaves

Strawberry Girl by Lois Lenski
Taran Wanderer by Lloyd Alexander
The Adventures of Huckleberry Finn by Mark Twain
The All-of-a-Kind Family by Sydney Taylor
The Amazing, Impossible Erie Canal by Cheryl Harness
The Bears on Hemlock Mountain by Alice Dalgliesh and Helen Sewell
The Bobbsey Twins series by Laura Lee Hope
The Boxcar Children series by Gertrude Chandler Warner
The Boyhood Diary of Theodore Roosevelt by Theodore Roosevelt and Shelley Swanson Sateren
The Courage of Sarah Noble by Jean Lee Latham
The Cricket in Times Square by George Selden
The Dragon's Hoard by Mell Eight
The Family Under the Bridge by Natalie Savage Carlson
The Five Little Peppers series by Margaret Sidney
The Hardy Boys series by Franklin W. Dixon
The Hundred Dresses by Eleanor Estes
The Little Prince by Antoine de Saint-Exupéry
The Phantom Tollbooth by Norton Juster and Jules Feiffer
The Saturdays by Elizabeth Enright
The Sword in the Tree by Clyde Robert Bulla and Bruce Bowles
The Trumpet of the Swan by E. B. White and Fred Marcellino
The Twenty-One Balloons by William Pene du Bois
The Wind in the Willows by Kenneth Grahame
Three Young Pilgrims by Cheryl Harness
Todd and Christy series by Robin Jones Gunn
Treasures of the Snow by Patricia St. John
Two Collars by Jeri Massi
"We Were There" series by Alida Sims Malkus and Leonard Vosburgh
Where the Red Fern Grows by Wilson Rawls
Winnie the Pooh by A. A. Milne, illustrated by Ernest H. Shepard
Winter Cottage by Carol Ryrie Brink
Young John Quincy by Cheryl Harness

> Fairy tales are more than true; not because they tell us that dragons exist, but because they tell us that dragons can be beaten.
> —Neil Gaiman

Must-Reads for Middle School Years

A Girl of the Limberlost by Gene Stratton-Porter
A Little Princess by Frances Hodgson Burnett
A Swiftly Tilting Planet by Madeleine L'Engle
A Wind in the Door by Madeleine L'Engle
A Wrinkle in Time by Madeleine L'Engle
Across Five Aprils by Irene Hunt

Adam of the Road by Elizabeth Janet Gray
Alice in Wonderland by Lewis Carroll
All Creatures Great and Small by James Herriott
Amos Fortune: Free Man by Elizabeth Yates
An Acceptable Time by Madeleine L'Engle
Anne of Green Gables series by L. M. Montgomery
Are You There, God? It's Me, Margaret by Judy Blume
Beautiful Joe by Margaret Marshall Saunders and Hezekiah Butterworth
Ben-Hur: A Tale of the Christ by Lewis Wallace
Bertie's War by Barbara Blakey
Black Beauty by Anna Sewell
Call It Courage by Armstrong Sperry
Canterwood Crest series by Jessica Burkhart
Cheaper by the Dozen by Frank B. Gilbreth and Ernestine Gilbreth Carey
Crispin: The Cross of Lead by Avi
Donna Parker series by Marcia Martin
Dork Diaries series by Rachel Renée Russell
Elsie Dinsmore series by Martha Finley
Emily Byrd Starr series by L. M. Montgomery
Gentle Ben by Walt Morey
Give Me Liberty by L. M. Elliott
Indian Captive: The Story of Mary Jemison by Lois Lenski
Indian in the Cupboard by Lynne Reid Banks
Island of the Blue Dolphins by Scott O'Dell
Jo's Boys by Louisa May Alcott
Johnny Tremaine by Esther Hoskins Forbes
Julie of the Wolves by Jean Craighead George and John Schoenherr
Just David by Eleanor H. Porter
Little Men by Louisa May Alcott
Little Women by Louisa May Alcott
Many Waters by Madeleine L'Engle
Number the Stars by Lois Lowry
On the Runway series by Melody Carlson
Paddle-to-the-Sea by Holling C. Holling
Rascal by Sterling North
Redwall series by Brian Jacques
Rifles for Watie by Harold Keith
Roll of Thunder, Hear My Cry by Mildred D. Taylor
Rose in Bloom by Louisa May Alcott
Sounder by William H. Armstrong
Summer of the Monkeys by Wilson Rawls
Swiss Family Robinson by Johann Wyss
The Boy Who Harnessed the Wind by William Kamkwamba, Bryan Mealer, et al.
The Bridge to Terabithia by Katherine Paterson and Donna Diamond
The Bronze Bow by Elizabeth George Speare
The Call of the Wild by Jack London
The Chronicles of Narnia by C. S. Lewis
The Door in the Wall by Marguerite de Angeli

The Eagle of the Ninth by Rosemary Sutcliff
The Girl of the Limberlost by Gene Stratton-Porter
The Giver by Lois Lowry
The Golden Goblet by Eloise Jarvis McGraw
The Incredible Journey by Sheila Burnford
The Little White Horse by Elizabeth Goudge
The Mother-Daughter Book Club series by Heather Vogel Frederick
The Railway Children by Edith Nesbit
The Secret Garden by Frances Hodgson Burnett
The Sign of the Beaver by Elizabeth George Speare
The Singing Tree by Kate Seredy
The Story Girl by L. M. Montgomery
The Story of D-Day by Bruce Bliven, Jr.
The Summer of the Swans by Betsy Byars
The Wind in the Willows by Kenneth Grahame
The Witch of Blackbird Pond by Elizabeth George Speare
The Wolves of Willoughby Chase by Joan Aiken
The Yearling by Marjorie Kinnan Rawlings
This Is Our Constitution by Khizr Khan
Three Girls and a Secret by Rene Guillot
Through the Looking Glass by Lewis Carroll
Trixie Belden series by Julie Campbell
Tuck Everlasting by Natalie Babbit
Twice Upon a Time by Wendy Mass
Under the Lilacs by Louisa May Alcott
Up a Road Slowly by Irene Hunt
Words by Heart by Ouida Sebestyen

There is more treasure in books than in all the pirate's loot on Treasure Island and best of all, you can enjoy these riches every day of your life.

—Walt Disney

Must-Reads for High School Years

A Girl of the Limberlost by Gene Porter
A Tale of Two Cities by Charles Dickens
A Tree Grows in Brooklyn by Betty Smith
All Quiet on the Western Front by Erich Remarque
Animal Farm by George Orwell
Anna Karenina by Leo Tolstoy
Around the World in Eighty Days by Jules Verne
Brave New World by Aldous Huxley
David Copperfield by Charles Dickens
Emma by Jane Austin
Gone with the Wind by Margaret Mitchell
Grapes of Wrath by John Steinbeck

Great Expectations by Charles Dickens
Hamlet by William Shakespeare
Hannah Coulter by Wendell Berry
Jane Eyre by Charlotte Bronte
Julius Caesar by William Shakespeare
Kidnapped by Robert Louis Stevenson
Mara, Daughter of the Nile by Eloise Jarvis McGraw
Moby Dick by Herman Melville
Mrs. Mike by Benedict Freedman and Nancy Freedman
My Name Is Ahser Lev by Chaim Potok
My Side of the Mountain by Jean Craighead George
Nineteen Eighty-Four by George Orwell
Of Mice and Men by John Steinbeck
Of Plymouth Plantation by William Bradford
Oliver Twist by Charles Dickens
Out of the Silent Planet by C. S. Lewis
Perelandra by C. S. Lewis
Pride and Prejudice by Jane Austen
Promises on the Wind by Irene Hunt
Quo Vadis by Henryk Sienkiewicz
Romeo and Juliet by William Shakespeare
Sense and Sensibility by Jane Austen
Silas Marner by George Eliot
That Hideous Strength by C. S. Lewis
The Adventures of Sherlock Holmes by Sir Arthur Conan Doyle
The Chosen by Chaim Potok
The Good Earth by Pearl S. Buck
The Great Gatsby by F. Scott Fitzgerald
The Guernsey Literary and Potato Peel Pie Society by Mary Ann Schaffer and Annie Barrows
The Heart of Darkness by Joseph Conrad
The Keeper of the Bees by Gene Stratton-Porter
The Last of the Mohicans by James Fenimore Cooper
The Lord of the Rings by J. R. R. Tolkien
The Man Who Was Thursday by G. K. Chesterton
The Merchant of Venice by William Shakespeare
The Old Man and the Sea by Ernest Hemingway
The Once and Future King by T. H. White
The Red Badge of Courage by Stephen Crane
The Robe by Lloyd C. Douglas
The Scarlet Letter by Nathanael Hawthorne
The Scarlet Pimpernel by Baroness Orczy
The Selection series by Kiera Cass
The Song of the Lark by Willa Cather
The Tide in the Attic by Aleid Van Rhijn
To Kill a Mockingbird by Harper Lee
Tortured for Christ by Richard Wurmbrand
Treasure Island by Robert Louis Stevenson
Uncle Tom's Cabin by Harriet Beecher Stowe

Watership Down by Richard Adams
Wuthering Heights by Emily Bronte

A book is a garden, an orchard, a storehouse, a party, a company
by the way, a counselor, a multitude of counselors.

—Charles Baudelaire

Biographies for Elementary and Middle School

Benjamin Franklin by Ingri and Edgar D'Aulaire
Betsy Ross, Designer of Our Flag by Ann Weil
Bring Me Some Apples and I'll Make You a Pie by Robin Gourley
Coming Home by Floyd Cooper
Dizzy by Jonah Winter
Fort Mose by Glennette Tilley Turner
Gladys Aylward: The Little Woman by Gladys Aylward
Helen Keller by Margaret Davidson
Heroes of History series
Julia Ward Howe, Girl of Old New York by Jean Brown Wagoner
Little Melba and Her Big Trombone by Katheryn Russell-Brown
Marie Curie and the Discovery of Radium by Ann E. Stineke
Mary Todd Lincoln: Girl of the Bluegrass by Katharine E. Wilkie
Molly, by Golly! by Dianne Ochiltree
Musical Genius: A Story about Wolfgang Amadeus Mozart by Barbara Allman
Narrative of the Life of Frederick Douglass by Frederick Douglass
Neil Armstrong – Young Flyer by Montrew Dunham
Sergeant York by John Perry
Spiritual Lives of the Great Composers by Patrick Kavanough
Stealing Home: The Story of Jackie Robinson by Barry Denenberg
The Story of George Washington Carver by Eva Moore
The Wright Brothers: Pioneers of American Aviation by Quentin Reynolds
Thomas Edison, Young Inventor by Sue Guthridge

Not all readers are leaders but all leaders are readers.

—President Harry Truman

Biographies for High School

A Chance to Die by Elisabeth Elliot
A Man Called Peter by Catherine Marshall
A Passion for the Impossible: The Life of Lilias Trotter by Miriam Rockness
A Severe Mercy by Sheldon Vanauken
Anne Frank: The Diary of a Young Girl by Anne Frank
Christy by Catherine Marshall

Churchill by Paul Johnson
Evidence Not Seen by Darlene Rose
God's Smuggler by Brother Andrew
If I Perish by Esther Ahn Kim
L'Abri by Edith Schaeffer
Night by Elie Wiesel
Surprised by Joy by C. S. Lewis
The Hiding Place by Corrie Ten Boom
Through Gates of Splendor by Elisabeth Elliot
Tolkien and the Great War by John Garth
Unbroken by Laura Hillenbrand
Up from Slavery by Booker T. Washington

What a blessing it is to love books as I love them; to be able to converse with the dead and to live amidst the unreal!
—Thomas Babington Macaulay

Poetry

A Child's Book of Poems by Gyo Fujikawa
A Child's Garden of Verses by Robert Louis Stevenson
Carver: A Life in Poems by Marilyn Nelson
Diary of an Old Soul by George MacDonald
Favorite Poems Old and New selected by Helen Ferris
Jabberwocky and Other Nonsense: The Collected Poems of Lewis Carroll
Leaves of Grass by Walt Whitman
National Geographic Book of Nature Poetry by J. Patrick Lewis
Now We Are Six by A. A. Milne
Out of the Dust by Karen Hesse
Poems by Christina Rossetti
Poetry for Kids by Robert Frost
Poetry for Young People by Emily Dickinson edited by Frances Schoonmaker Bolin
Poetry for Young People by Walt Whitman edited by Jonathan Levin
Sonnets from the Portuguese by Elizabeth Barrett Browning
The Best Loved Poems of the American People by Hazel Felleman and Frank Allen
The Best Poems of the English Language by Harold Bloom (Editor)
The Giving Tree by Shel Silverstein
The Golden Books Family Treasury of Poetry selected by Louis Untermeyer
The Oxford Illustrated Book of American Children's Poems edited by Donald Hall
The Random House Book of Poetry for Children by Jack Prelutsky
The Road Not Taken and Other Poems by Robert Frost
When We Were Very Young by A. A. Milne
When You Are Old: Early Poems and Fairy Tales by William Butler Yeats
Where the Sidewalk Ends by Shel Silverstein
Winter Poems selected by Barbara Rogasky

Books for the Holidays

Preschool and Young Readers

Cranberry Thanksgiving by Wende and Harry Devlin
Give Thanks to the Lord by Karma Wilson
Over the River and Through the Wood by Lydia Maria Child
Sharing the Bread: An Old Fashioned Thanksgiving Story by Pat Miller
Squanto's Journey: The Story of the First Thanksgiving by Joseph Bruchac
Thank You, Sarah: The Woman Who Saved Thanksgiving by Laurie Halse Anderson
Thanks for Thanksgiving by Julie Markes
Thanksgiving in the Woods by Phyllis Alsdurf, illustrated by Jenny Lovlie
Thanksgiving Is Here by Diane Goode
Thanksgiving on Thursday (The Magic Tree House Series) by Mary Pope Osborne
The Story of the Pilgrims by Katharine Ross and Carolyn Croll
The Thanksgiving Story by Alice Dalgliesh
Christmas in the Manger by Nola Buck
Christmas in the Trenches by John McCutcheon
How the Grinch Stole Christmas by Dr. Seuss
Humphrey's First Christmas by Carol Heyer
The Christmas Cat by Efner Tudor Holmes, illustrated by Tasha Tudor
The Christmas Wish by Lori Evert
The Crippled Lamb by Max Lucado
The Miracle of Jonathan Toomey by Susan Wojciechowski and P.J. Lynch
The Mysterious Star by Joanne Marxhausen
The Year of the Perfect Christmas Tree: An Appalachian Story by Gloria Houston and Barbara Cooney
Who Is Coming to Our House by Joseph Slate and Ashley Wolff
Apple Pie 4th of July by Janet S. Wong
If You Sailed on the Mayflower in 1620 by Ann McGovern
The Berenstain Bears God Bless Our Country by Mike Berenstain
The Fourth of July Story by Alice Dalgliesh, illustrated by Marie Nonnast
The Night Before the Fourth of July by Natasha Wing
The Story of America's Birthday by Patricia Pingry

Middle School

A Christmas Carol by Charles Dickens
Christmas in My Heart anthology series by Joe Wheeler
Jotham's Journey by Arnold Ytreeide
The Best Christmas Pageant Ever by Barbara Robinson
The Nativity illustrated by Julie Vivas
Two from Galilee: The Story of Mary and Joseph by Marjorie Holmes
A Is for America by Devin Scillian
Poems and Songs Celebrating America by Ann Braybrooks

Books Offering Hope and Therefore Growth

Not My Will, But Thine by Neal A. Maxwell
Stepping Heavenward by Elizabeth Prentiss
The Great Divorce by C. S. Lewis
The Scent of Water by Elizabeth Goudge
The Screwtape Letters by C. S. Lewis

You can never get a cup of tea large enough or a book long enough to suit me.
—C. S. Lewis

APPENDIX B
Recipes from the McLeod Kitchen

The Best Rice You Have Ever Tasted...You're Welcome!

5-1/2 cups chicken broth, divided
1 cup golden raisins
6 tbl. butter, divided
1 cup uncooked wild rice
1 cup uncooked brown rice
1 cup sliced or slivered almonds
1/4 tsp salt
1/4 tsp pepper

Directions:

In a small saucepan, bring 1/2 cup broth to a boil. Remove from the heat; add the raisins and set aside. Do not drain.

In a large saucepan, bring 3 cups of broth and 2 tbl. butter to a boil; add wild rice. Cover and simmer for 55-60 minutes or until the rice is tender. Check it often and add more chicken broth if necessary.

Meanwhile, in another saucepan, combine the brown rice, 2 tbl. butter and remaining broth. Bring to a boil. Reduce heat; cover and simmer for 35-40 minutes or until rice is tender. You may need to drain or add more broth as you check it often.

In a skillet, sauté the almonds in remaining butter until lightly browned. In a serving bowl, combine the wild rice, brown rice, raisins, almonds, salt and pepper. Serve and savor!

Magic Meat Loaf

4 eggs, slightly beaten
23 ounces tomato juice
1 large onion, finely chopped
2 celery ribs, finely chopped
1/4 cup of finely chopped carrots
2-1/4 cups seasoned bread crumbs
1 envelope dry onion soup mix
1 tsp. ground pepper
4 pounds ground beef
1/2 cup ketchup
1/4 cup brown sugar
2 tbl. prepared mustard

Directions:

In a very large bowl, combine the eggs, tomato juice, onions, celery, carrots, bread crumbs, soup mix and pepper. Crumble beef over mixture and mix well with hands.

Shape into 2 loaves; place each loaf in a greased loaf pan. Bake uncovered at 350 degrees for 45 minutes.

Meanwhile, combine the ketchup, brown sugar and mustard. Spread over the loaves and bake 15 minutes longer or until a meat thermometer reads 160 degrees.

I call this *magic* meat loaf because it disappears before your very eyes!

Special Delivery Chicken

2 cups (16 oz.) sour cream
1 can (10-3/4 oz.) condensed cream of chicken soup, undiluted
2 teaspoons poppy seeds
2-1/2 cups cubed cooked chicken
1-3/4 cups butter-flavored cracker crumbs (about 36 crackers)
1/2 cup butter, melted

Directions:

In a bowl, combine the sour cream, soup and poppy seeds. Stir in chicken. Pour into a greased 11x7x2-inch baking dish. Combine the cracker crumbs and butter; sprinkle over the top. Bake uncovered at 350 degrees for 25-30 minutes until bubbling. I generally double this recipe for great leftovers!

McLeod Family Broccoli Casserole

1 lbs. fresh broccoli, cut into florets
1 can (10-3/4 ounces) condensed cream of mushroom soup, undiluted
1/2 cup mayonnaise
1/2 cup shredded cheddar cheese
1 tbl. lemon juice
1 cup crushed cheese-flavored snack crackers

Directions:

Place 1 inch of water and broccoli in saucepan; bring to a boil. Reduce heat; cover and simmer for 5 to 8 minutes or just until crisp tender. Drain and place in a greased 1-qt. baking dish.

In a small bowl, combine the soup, mayonnaise, cheese, and lemon juice. Pour over broccoli. Sprinkle with crushed crackers. Bake uncovered at 350 degrees for 25 to 30 minutes or until heated through.

Carol's Famous Corn Pudding

1 bag frozen corn
1 can creamed corn
3 eggs, beaten
1 cup milk
2 tbl. flour
1 tsp. salt
3 tbl. sugar
3 tbl. butter

Directions:

Combine the eggs, milk, flour, salt and sugar together well until there are no lumps. Then, add the frozen corn and the creamed corn. Pour into a greased casserole dish and dot with butter. Bake at 350 degrees, stirring every 15 minutes, for one hour. The best! Make a double portion!

Christmas Morning Egg Casserole

1 pound hot or mild sausage browned and drained
8 eggs
1 cup grated sharp cheese
2 cups milk
1 tsp salt
1 tsp dry mustard
1 dash tobacco sauce
1 dash Worcestershire sauce
4 slices of bread (preferably white) cubed

Directions:

Beat eggs, milk and seasonings together.

Layer sausage, bread crumbs and cheese and then pour the egg mixture over it all. Let sit in the refrigerator overnight and bake it in the morning at 350 degrees for 45-60 minutes. Serve with a fruit salad and sweet rolls.

Thanksgiving Pretzel Topped Sweet Potatoes

2 cups chopped pretzel rods
1 cup chopped pecans
1 cup fresh or frozen cranberries
1 cup packed brown sugar
1 cup butter, divided
1 can (2.5 pounds) sweet potatoes, drained
1 can evaporated milk
1/2 cup sugar
1 tsp. vanilla extract

Directions:

In a large bowl, combine the pretzels, pecans, cranberries, brown sugar and 1/2 cup butter; set aside.

In a large bowl, beat the sweet potatoes until smooth. Add the milk, sugar, vanilla and remaining butter; beat until well-blended.

Spoon into greased shallow 2-qt. baking dish; sprinkled with pretzel mixture. Bake uncovered at 350 degrees for 25-30 minutes or until the edges are bubbly. Yum!

March Madness Nuts and Bolts

4 cups Cheerios
4 cups bite-size Shredded Wheat
4 cups pretzel sticks
3 cups salted peanuts
3/4 cup butter
3 tbl. Worcestershire sauce
1 tsp. each celery salt, onion salt, garlic salt and paprika

Directions:

In a large bowl, combine cereals, pretzels and nuts. In a saucepan, melt butter and add seasonings. Pour over cereal mix and toss to coat. Spread evenly over 2 cookies sheets. Bake at 250 degrees for 1 hour, stirring every 15 minutes. Cool and store in an airtight container.

Carol's Pumpkin Cookies

1 cup butter, softened
2/3 cup packed brown sugar
1/3 cup sugar
1 large egg
1 tsp. vanilla extract
1 cup canned pumpkin
2 cups all-purpose flour
1-1/2 tsp. ground cinnamon
1 tsp. baking soda
1/2 tsp. salt
1/4 tsp. baking powder
1 cup chopped walnuts

Frosting:

1/4 cup butter, softened
4 ounces cream cheese, softened
2 cups confectioners' sugar
1-1/2 tsp. vanilla extract

Directions:

In a large bowl, cream butter and sugars until light and fluffy. Beat in egg and vanilla. Add pumpkin; mix well. Combine the flour, cinnamon, baking soda, salt and baking powder; gradually add to creamed mixture and mix well. Stir in walnuts.

Drop by rounded tablespoons 2 in. apart onto greased baking sheets. Bake at 350 degrees for 8-10 minutes or until edges are lightly browned. Remove to wire racks to cool completely.

In a small bowl, beat the frosting ingredients until light and fluffy. Frost cookies. Store in an airtight container in the refrigerator.

McLeod Family Oat-rageous Chocolate Chip Cookies

1/2 cup butter, softened
1/2 cup creamy peanut butter
1/2 cup sugar
1/3 cup packed brown sugar
1 large egg, room temperature
1/2 tsp. vanilla extract
1 cup all-purpose flour
1/2 cup quick-cooking oats
1 tsp. baking soda
1/4 tsp. salt
1 cup semisweet chocolate chips

Directions:

In a large bowl, cream butter, peanut butter and sugars; beat in egg and vanilla. Combine flour, oats, baking soda and salt. Add to the creamed mixture and mix well. Stir in chocolate chips. Drop by rounded tablespoons onto ungreased baking sheet. Bake at 350 degrees for 10-12 minutes or until lightly browned.

ABOUT THE AUTHOR

The president and CEO of Carol McLeod Ministries, Carol McLeod is a popular speaker at women's conferences and retreats. She is the author of a dozen books, including *Vibrant: Developing a Deep and Abiding Joy for All Seasons*; *Significant: Becoming a Woman of Unique Purpose, True Identity, and Irrepressible Hope*; *StormProof: Weathering Life's Tough Times*; *Guide Your Mind, Guard Your Heart, Grace Your Tongue*; *Joy for All Seasons*; *Holy Estrogen*; and *Defiant Joy*.

Carol hosts a twice weekly podcast, *A Jolt of Joy!* on the Charisma Podcast Network, and a weekly podcast, *Significant*. Her weekly blog, *Joy for the Journey*, has been named in the Top 50 Faith Blogs for Women. Carol also writes a weekly column in *Ministry Today*.

She has written several devotionals for YouVersion, including "21 Days to Beat Depression," which has touched the lives of nearly one million people around the world. Her teaching DVD *The Rooms of a Woman's Heart* won the prestigious Telly Award for excellence in religious programming.

Carol was also the first women's chaplain at Oral Roberts University and served as chaplain on the university's Alumni Board of Directors for many years.

Carol has been married to her college sweetheart, Craig, for more than forty years and is the mother of five children in heaven and five children on earth. Carol and Craig also happily answer to "Marmee and Pa" for their captivating grandchildren.